Young Writers 2005 POETRY

CW00631250

PLAYGROUND

Let your creativity flow...

ode
limerick
haiku
rhyme
ballad

- Expressions From The Midlands Vol II

Edited by Liz Thornbury

 Young**Writers**

First published in Great Britain in 2006 by:
Young Writers
Remus House
Coltsfoot Drive
Peterborough
PE2 9JX
Telephone: 01733 890066
Website: www.youngwriters.co.uk

All Rights Reserved

© *Copyright Contributors 2005*

SB ISBN 1 84602 361 0

Foreword

Young Writers was established in 1991 and has been passionately devoted to the promotion of reading and writing in children and young adults ever since. The quest continues today. Young Writers remains as committed to the fostering of burgeoning poetic and literary talent as ever.

This year's Young Writers competition has proven as vibrant and dynamic as ever and we are delighted to present a showcase of the best poetry from across the UK. Each poem has been carefully selected from a wealth of *Playground Poets* entries before ultimately being published in this, our thirteenth primary school poetry series.

Once again, we have been supremely impressed by the overall high quality of the entries we have received. The imagination, energy and creativity which has gone into each young writer's entry made choosing the best poems a challenging and often difficult but ultimately hugely rewarding task - the general high standard of the work submitted amply vindicating this opportunity to bring their poetry to a larger appreciative audience.

We sincerely hope you are pleased with our final selection and that you will enjoy *Playground Poets - Expressions From The Midlands Vol II* for many years to come.

Contents

Jarred Raybould (10)	35
Jack Roestenburg (11)	35
Emily Banks (9)	35
Charlotte Connolly (10)	36
Adam Greer (10)	36
Andrew Franklin (11)	37
Freya Cleasby (9)	37
Matthew Lovatt (9)	37
Oliver Stanlake (9)	38
Megan Challinor (10)	38
Sammy Cooper (9)	38
Rupert Thomas	39
Megan Jenks (9)	39
David Edge (9)	39
Daniel Clarke (9)	40
David Anderson (9)	40
Joshua Key (9)	40
Lois Calder (9)	41
Bethany Lee (9)	41
Lauren Hough (9)	41
Antonia Bailey (10)	42
Jack Smith (9)	42
Clare Lester (9)	42
Jake Triggs (9)	43
Eleanor Coates (9)	43
Connor Smith (9)	43

Barrow CE Primary School, Broseley

Alice Cotton (9)	44
Joseph Anderson (10)	44
James Challenor (10)	45
Nicole Wellsford (10)	45
Laura-Beth Bowen (10)	46
Jordan Clarke (10)	47

Clive CE Primary School, Shrewsbury

Heather Simcock (8)	47
Rory Bothwell (10)	48
Robert Hughes (8)	48
Henry Walker (9)	48
Nina M Andersen Smith (10)	49

Rachel Sharp (8)	64
Darcie-May Luckman (9)	64
Victoria Boulton (9)	64
Courtney Heathcote (9)	65
Alisha Tomson (8)	65
Chelsea Reece (9)	65
Chloe Denniss (8)	66
Tammy Tomlinson (8)	66
Treasure Edwards (8)	66
Rebecca Plant (7)	67
Aysha Longdon (8)	67
Caitlin Foster (7)	68
Lauren Robb (7)	69
Kyle Parsons (7)	69
Elliot Jones (8)	70
Sarah Corbett (7)	70
Sam McNamara (7)	71
Timothy Ratcliffe (11)	71
Jessica Wheatley (10)	71
Anna Boulton (10)	72
Robert Kempson (10)	72
Mark Moffat (9)	72
David Li (7)	73
Adrian Wood (11)	73
Joseph Bush (10)	73
Alice Holmes (10)	74
Cally Sadler (10)	74
Julie Phillips (10)	75
Kelcie Oakley (10)	75

Haberdashers' Redcap School, Hereford

Abigail Carruthers (9)	76
Sophie Wallis (10)	76
Elizabeth Keir (10)	77
Roisin Massam-Vallely (9)	77
Kathryn Subak-Sharpe (10)	78
Julia Watkinson (10)	78
Florence Churchward (10)	79
Emily Beckett (9)	79
Sophie Nash (9)	79

Longden CE Primary School, Shrewsbury

Francesca South (10)	80
Adam Wagstaff (9)	80
Emily-Jane Mitchell (9)	81
Abigail Nixon (10)	81
Rebecca Bruce (10)	82
Charlie Forth (10)	82
Meagan Roberts (11)	83
Sophie Rowson (9)	83
Jake Roberts (10)	83
James Brayne (11)	84
Jessica Cox (9)	84
Ellie Jenkins (10)	84
Holly Linford (11)	85
Lewis Jowett (10)	85
Daniel Rintoul (9)	86
Joel Pugh (9)	86
Thomas Lear (9)	87
John Merrick (9)	87
Kathryn Adams (10)	88

Milverton Primary School, Leamington Spa

Lydia Ungless (7)	88
Cameron Love (10)	88
Sophie Rowe (7)	89
Natalie Gould (9)	89
Neena Abdullah (11)	90
Molly Minshull (10)	90
Anne Devereux (9)	91
Aidan Bradbury (10)	91
Heidi Roberts (9)	92
Lauren Pugh (10)	92
Gabrielle Calvert (9)	92
Hannah Pope (10)	93
Oliver Murray (10)	93
Rory Barber (9)	94
David Fairbairn (9)	94
Yousef Hanif (11)	95
Abigail Watt (9)	95
Harry Conway (10)	96
George Lambert (10)	96

Maisie Tudge (9)	97
Alexander Bennell (9)	97
Luis Alarcon (9)	98

Our Lady & St Werburgh's RC School, Newcastle

Joanna Lam (10)	99
Katie Bullock (10)	99
Sophie Bunting (10)	100
Rachel Sherwin (10)	100
Ruairidh McKenna (10)	101
Harriet Allbutt (10)	101
Holly Payne (10)	102
Megan Nolan (10)	102
Charlotte Counter (10)	103
Jessica Scally (10)	103
Jade Ely (10)	104
Marisha Monaghan (11)	104
Megan McCoy (10)	105

Queens CE Junior School, Nuneaton

Tayyibah Patel (10)	105
Amani Ismail (11)	106
Alison House	106
Alison Hughes	107
Gemma Campbell	107
Marcus Holt (10)	107
Jessica Tandy (10)	108
Amy Marshall (10)	108
Jamie Slack (10)	109
Connor Fletcher	109
Umar Aswat (10)	110
Jack Jones	110
Adil Shaikh	111
Leah Stringer	111
Rizwaan Dawood	111
Gemma Mann	112
Jack Gwilliam (10)	112
Lewis Wilkinson (11)	112
Saddaf Caratella (10)	113
Stephanie Mason (11)	113
Gemma Nicholson (10)	113

Charlotte Richards (7)	129
Kkyan Dunét (8)	130
Tonicha Southern (8)	131
Ben Cross (8)	132
Jordana Thatcher (8)	133
Poppy McMulkin (8)	134
Rebecca Hutchings (7)	135
Rebecca Prentice (8)	136
Matthew Dale (7)	137
Tyler Young (7)	138
Matilda Markantonakis (7)	139
Katy Nash (7)	140
Hannah Wright (7)	141

St Benedict's Catholic Primary School, Atherstone

Evangeline Ford (10)	141
Kieran Forsyth (10)	142
Rachel Burns (9)	142
Tyler Beeson (9)	142
Tiana Cavanagh	143
Ola Wrobel (10)	143
Heather Lees (9)	144
Daniel Morton (9)	144
Alicia Winfield-O'Hare (9)	145
Shannen Strugnell (9)	145
Ryan Daly (9)	145
Jonathan Strugnell (9)	146
David Tremlett (9)	146
Abbie Palmer (9)	146
Lucy Turner (9)	147
Jamie Dorman (9)	147
Holly Paton (10)	148
Zak Yates (9)	148
Harriet Littlewood (9)	149
Patrick Davey (9)	149
Rosie Holland (9)	150
Chloe Smith (9)	150
Sophie Skelcher (9)	151

St Francis Xavier's RC Primary School, Hereford

| Caitlin Price (9) | 151 |

Daniel Waite (10)	172
Helen Stevenson (11)	173
Rachel Beasley-Suffolk (10)	174

Whittington CE Primary School, Worcester

Zoe Evans (10)	174
Alice Fisher (10)	175
Rory Wilkinson (10)	176
Daniel Burch (10)	177
Tom Massingham (10)	178
Ryan Upson (10)	179
Jade Morris (10)	180
Josh Clayton (10)	181
Charlotte Mitchell (10)	182
Emma Sheldon (10)	183
Kieran Rodway (10)	184
Paige Jones (10)	185

Wigmore Primary School, Wigmore

Jodie Kerton (9)	185
James Phillips (9)	186
Lexine Maughfling (10)	186
Hannah Mason (10)	187
Alex Edwards (10)	188
Jamie Bufton (9)	188
Thomas Stevens (9)	189
Hannah Segar (8)	189
Zak Kyriakou (9)	190
Sam Boxhall (8)	190
Kirsty Ann Gibbs Mellings (9)	191
Jake Pontifex-Price (8)	191
Rhys Brown (9)	192
Jack Lewin (8)	192
Emma Crooke (10)	193
Lucy Brown (10)	193
Siri Lewis (10)	194
Sophie Hatt (8)	194
Lucy Willmett (10)	195
Olivia Edwards (8)	195
Phillipa Yarranton (10)	196
Lucy Evans (8)	196

The Poems

No More Left Here

A wave is coming to hit us,
Coming, coming, don't know what to do,
It's Boxing Day and no word,
Having turkey, then it popped up,
A wave hit Sri Lanka.

Crashing, bashing cars away,
A girl hangs onto a post, screaming for her life.
Millions of litres of water,
Rushing across everything in its path,
Sweeping people and houses away.

People shouting, people screaming,
No help coming here today.
People dying from raging waters.
What to do at a time like this!

Ruins are left from water,
Lives and people wrecked,
Dirt swiped in from the south,
Houses washed away to sea.

Lives are ruined! Aeroplanes are coming to help,
Not much left from the houses, 'No more left here'.
No people here now,
Waves washed civilisation away
Nothing here but water!

Nothing to do because of the water,
No playing, nowhere to live, nothing to eat,
No pubs, nothing! No!

Connor Howen (9)

Inside The Pirates' Chest

Inside the pirates' chest we found;
Ten red diamonds sparkling in the light,
Nine golden necklaces gleaming,
Eight golden crowns shining,
Seven silver bracelets glowing in the sun,
Six grinning masks fading,
Five bronze emeralds rusting,
Four whitish-purple shells cracking,
Three black eye patches knotting,
Two wine bottles smashing
And one ancient map marked with an 'X'.

Molly Croft (7)
Barnfields Primary School, Stafford

Inside The Pirate Chest

Inside the pirate chest we found;
Ten bronze plates smashing,
Nine golden diamonds breaking,
Eight wine bottles cracking,
Seven silver bracelets rusting,
Six black eye patches resting,
Five shiny silver necklaces sparkling,
Four wet, gold coins fading,
Three golden emeralds singing,
Two golden ruby rings glistening
And one ancient map marked with an 'X'.

Richard Leech (7)
Barnfields Primary School, Stafford

Inside The Pirate Chest

Inside the pirate chest we found;
Ten golden plates smashing,
Nine silver diamonds shining,
Eight bones crunching,
Seven wet gold coins rusting,
Six parrots speaking and their feathers glowing,
Five wine bottles popping,
Four seaweed plants dying,
Three bronze bracelets spinning,
Two shells wriggling
And one ancient map marked with an 'X'.

Emily Jackson (7)
Barnfields Primary School, Stafford

Inside The Pirate Chest

Inside the pirate chest we found;
Ten polished gemstones glistening,
Nine opal necklaces fading,
Eight silver swords breaking,
Seven mini chests rusting,
Six jewelled crowns cracking,
Five black eye patches knotting,
Four brown pirate masks grinning,
Three white skeletons snapping,
Two magic lamps glowing
And one ancient map marked with an 'X'.

Helena Organ (7)
Barnfields Primary School, Stafford

The Massive Super Slide

Listening carefully to instructions,
Struggling, slipping up the rope,
Climbing up to the very top,
Thinking, *yes, I'm there.*
Waiting for the man to say, 'Ready, steady, *go!*'
Saying, 'I am sad, I wish I could go again, oh!'

Nicola Blagg (7)
Barnfields Primary School, Stafford

Fear

Fear feels like you have got no friends
Fear looks like you're going to get beaten up
Fear smells like a sour onion making you cry
Fear is the colour of red burnt sausage
Fear tastes like hot spicy peppers
Fear sounds like scary music being played
Fear reminds me of my mum shouting really loud.

Jack Somerville (9)
Barnfields Primary School, Stafford

Sadness

Sadness smells like cheese rotting.
Sadness sounds like cats fighting.
Sadness reminds me of when I was born.
Sadness feels like a drill hurting me.
Sadness looks like rain falling.
Sadness is the colour blue.
Sadness tastes like apple pie.

Ashley Jones (8)
Barnfields Primary School, Stafford

Super Slide

Waiting, laughing, in the line.
Listening *very carefully* to the man.
Struggling up the tough rope.
Slipping on the steep hill.
Sitting up ready to go!
Falling, screaming, skidding,
Shouting, shaking, zooming,
Tumbling, whooshing, banging,
Crashing down the slide.
Rolling, flying and spinning in the air.
Crashing at the bottom!
Phew! I'm glad that's over!
Wow!

Owen Merriman (8)
Barnfields Primary School, Stafford

Wow That Looks Good!

Waiting impatiently to go up.
Listening to the man, excited wanting to go.
Struggling up the ladder, phew I'm up.
Slipping up the slide, this is hard work.
Sitting at the top, waiting for the man to say,'Go!'
Falling down the slippery slide, *argh!*
Sliding down and down, phew, I'm at the bottom.
Rolling off the slide, cool!
Crashing at the bottom, oh I want to go again.

Michael Taylor (7)
Barnfields Primary School, Stafford

Love

Love smells like sweet lavender.
Love looks like a blue sky and a sunny day.
Love feels like silk from silkworms.
Love reminds me of water trickling down a shiny stream.
Love's colour is gold, silver and bronze combined.
Love tastes like cakes of every kind.
Love sounds like birds singing.

Tom Barnard (8)
Barnfields Primary School, Stafford

Fear

Fear looks like dogs chasing cats.
Fear smells like burnt food at the bottom of the pan.
Fear is the colour of red and yellow and orange fire.
Fear tastes like onions that are sour.
Fear sounds like two clouds crashing to make a sound.
Fear reminds me of playing golf in the thunderstorms.
Fear feels like a dog's bitten me.

Amelia Whiting (8)
Barnfields Primary School, Stafford

Happiness

Happiness feels like soft rabbits' fur, toasty warm,
Happiness looks like a bright blue summer sky,
Happiness tastes like hot chocolate, one sip at a time,
Happiness smells like the scent of sweet tulips,
Happiness is the colour of the sun, a beautiful yellow,
Happiness reminds me of birds tweeting in the morning,
Happiness sounds like the tinkling of a stream.

Yasmin Duggal (8)
Barnfields Primary School, Stafford

Anger

Anger smells like rotten cabbages.
Anger looks like falling buildings.
Anger's colour is white from the bone.
Anger reminds me of two friends falling out.
Anger feels like someone stabbing me with a knife.
Anger sounds like a man screaming with pain.
Anger tastes like seawater.

Adam Bakewell (9)
Barnfields Primary School, Stafford

Sadness

Sadness reminds me when I get into a fight with my friends.
Sadness feels like a fire in my heart.
Sadness looks like a big red hole.
Sadness tastes like raw food.
Sadness smells like out of date water.
Sadness sounds like loud music.
Sadness' colour is a black sky.

Miles Harrison (8)
Barnfields Primary School, Stafford

Anger

Anger looks like a door slamming on me.
Anger's colour is the red of people's blood.
Anger reminds me of the world getting blown up.
Anger feels like my mouth getting ripped off.
Anger sounds like two armoured men fighting with swords.
Anger tastes like bonfires popping in my belly.
Anger smells like burnt vegetables.

Adam Davey (8)
Barnfields Primary School, Stafford

Hate

Hate makes me feel angry and sad.
Hate looks like red and grey.
Hate sounds like someone starting to cry.
Hate is coloured red and horrible.
Hate tastes horrible like onions.
Hate smells a little bit sweaty and hot.
Hate reminds me of when my dog died.

Aaron Mace (8)
Barnfields Primary School, Stafford

Sadness

Sadness feels like being upset.
Sadness looks like tears falling down your face.
Sadness tastes like drops of sour water in my mouth.
Sadness smells like soggy pears.
Sadness sounds like my head cracking open.
Sadness reminds me of when I was upset.
Sadness is black sky.

Rachel Peach (8)
Barnfields Primary School, Stafford

Love

Love feels like an arrow going through my heart.
Love reminds me of the day I got my dog.
Love is the colour pink.
Love smells like bread cooking.
Love looks like a heart curved in caramel.
Love tastes like chocolate Galaxy.
Love sounds like the sea.

Jack Calow (8)
Barnfields Primary School, Stafford

Hate

Hate looks like two people fighting.
Hate sounds like people screaming.
Hate is like a black hole.
Hate tastes like vegetables.
Hate smells like a burning barbecue.
Hate reminds me of being ill.
Hate feels cold.

Emma Tomkinson (8)
Barnfields Primary School, Stafford

Happiness

Happiness smells like strawberry milkshake,
Happiness is like a giant sneezing red hearts,
Happiness reminds me of a gigantic bowl of chocolate,
Happiness looks like a sparkling red rose,
Happiness tastes like an ice-cold lemonade
With a piece of lime on a blistering hot day,
Happiness feels like a pile of juicy red cherry tomatoes,
Happiness sounds like a cat purring.

Jade Edwards (8)
Barnfields Primary School, Stafford

Happiness

Happiness reminds me of my mum and dad getting married,
Happiness feels like a hot summer's day,
Happiness looks like a red rose during the day,
Happiness tastes like a cold, little drink,
Happiness smells like the topping of a cake,
Happiness is the colour of a red firework,
Happiness sounds like a dog barking happily.

Grace Hornby (8)
Barnfields Primary School, Stafford

Hate

Hate smells like rotten cheese and mouldy bread.
Hate reminds me of two people fighting.
Hate feels like your best friend has just betrayed you.
Hate looks like a friend has stolen something from you.
Hate sounds like two people screaming.
Hate is the colour of a deadly red.
Hate tastes like burnt food in my mouth.

Jake Nicholls (8)
Barnfields Primary School, Stafford

Fear

Fear smells like wet mud.
Fear looks like when you're on your own in a power cut.
Fear tastes like when you swallow seawater.
Fear sounds like someone is screaming.
Fear reminds me of the first time I went to school.
Fear feels like a monster in your closet.
Fear looks like a crashed plane.

Jack Thomas (9)
Barnfields Primary School, Stafford

Hate

Hate reminds me of World War II.
Hate feels like someone is jumping on you.
Hate looks like a really sad painting.
Hate sounds like the radio has been turned up too loud.
Hate is the colour of evil red paint.
Hate tastes like mouldy, burnt toast.
Hate smells like overdone cake.

Monica Walker (9)
Barnfields Primary School, Stafford

Hate

Hate tastes like rotten food,
Hate smells like fresh blood,
Hate reminds me of the sadness that it brings,
Hate feels like people have abandoned you,
Hate looks like horrible people,
Hate sounds like music that you don't like,
Hate is the colour black.

Alice Watterson (8)
Barnfields Primary School, Stafford

Happiness

Happiness looks like a great big smile.
Happiness tastes like Christmas pudding.
Happiness smells like fresh orange.
Happiness is orange and red.
Happiness reminds me of playing with my friends.
Happiness sounds like laughing.
Happiness feels like a warm, soft blanket.

James Harris (8)
Barnfields Primary School, Stafford

Fear

Fear is like the colour pitch-black when you close your eyes.
Fear tastes like blood when you bite your tongue.
Fear sounds like a woman screaming loudly.
Fear reminds me of a long and horrible nightmare.
Fear feels like a pile of snow that's just dropped on you.
Fear looks like someone falling off a bike.
Fear smells like food when it has gone mouldy.

Amber Wilkinson (9)
Barnfields Primary School, Stafford

I Am Scared

What can I see?
I see people scared and lonely.
I see mothers hanging onto their children.
A train came and I saw mothers saying goodbye.
I see a sad train driver sitting in the front.

What can I hear?
Scared mothers saying goodbye.
A train going from the city.
I hear the church bells ring.
Every child is leaving here.

What do I feel?
I feel heartbroken.
I don't feel safe.
I feel like I've been split in half
And that's what I feel, hear and see.

Danielle Woodward (8)
Barnfields Primary School, Stafford

The Apple Tree

Come on apple, come with me,
Come out of your apple tree.
Lovely coloured, bright and shiny,
When will you come and be mine.

Come on apple, come with me,
Come out of your apple tree.
It is time to say goodbye,
You are going in my pie.
Come on apple, come with me,
Come out of your apple tree.

Get the custard, get the plate,
You are delicious, really great!

Andrew Hall (10)
Barnfields Primary School, Stafford

I'm An Evacuee

I am an evacuee and this is what I see.
A lonely crowd, grey and brown, this is what I see.
The driver watching sadly as he waves a sorrowful goodbye.
Off he goes on his own very sad indeed.
Billets, billets everywhere, moaning people as they stare.
Gas masks on, gas masks off, weeping mothers with a cough.
Officers shouting, 'Off we come,' as the last of us look in shock.

Matthew Bamber (9)
Barnfields Primary School, Stafford

Anger

Anger reminds me of two tigers fighting,
Anger feels like a dangerous animal in Africa,
Anger smells like a bomb in a fight,
Anger looks like a green table on the floor,
Anger sounds like a chair cracking,
Anger tastes like a sour orange.

Lucy Cantrill (9)
Barnfields Primary School, Stafford

Love

Love looks like a love heart bursting with love and hugs.
Love feels like sweetness and happiness.
Love reminds me of people getting married.
Love reminds me of the colour pink.
Love smells like red and white roses.
Love sounds like the wind blowing silently.
Love tastes like lovely oozing chocolate.

Sophia Armstrong (8)
Barnfields Primary School, Stafford

What Happened To Me In World War II

'This country is now at war with Germany',
In my ear,
I could hear.
Church bells dinging.
Air raid sirens ringing.

I am at the station
All I hear is whistles blowing,
Bombs exploding.
Still in the distance,
In an instant
Moany Margaret echoing.

Children bobbing up,
In the misty atmosphere with gas masks.
Worried soldiers with tricky tasks.
In the swampy fields,
Men running around with mighty strength
And machine guns, with long length.

Children wailing,
Mothers paling.
Soldiers dying
Mothers crying
All this war
All this war
It will come to an end.

Laurat Zoaka (9)
Barnfields Primary School, Stafford

Autumn

The season's here.
There are conkers falling off trees.
Squirrels are out now.
The hedgehogs are coming out.
The leaves are different colours.

Georgia Cromwell (9)
Barnfields Primary School, Stafford

It's Terrible To Be An Evacuee

What can you see?
Children just as lonely as me
Holding their bags as if they'll never let go.
Families clinging to each other,
The train driver watching sadly as we board the train.

What can you hear?
The train driver blowing his whistle.
Mothers saying goodbye to their children,
Sounds like they may never see them again.
Time to leave, silence calls on everyone.

What do you smell?
The smell of steam as it leaves the train.
Hot sweaty bodies crushing together.
The cold air of winter rushing past.
The smell of war as bombs explode.

How do you feel?
Scared and lonely but quite safe now.
Very, very frightened without our mothers,
Like a timid mouse being chased by a cat.
Scared and cold and angry to be evacuated.

To be an evacuee is terrible of course
But it is for the best . . .

Gemma England (8)
Barnfields Primary School, Stafford

Autumn - Tanka

It's autumn again
Autumn leaves changing colours
The conkers falling
Little boys picking them up
It is now autumn again.

Tom Jackson (9)
Barnfields Primary School, Stafford

Bad War Night

I feel like things are spinning
With all those church bells ringing
Weeping noises, I feel so strange
Hoping that I will be back home again
Air raids, nervous, worried and cold
Kids and parents, young and old
Gas masks lying on the ground
All those noises, all those sounds
Soldiers passing in their cars
Some so sad, they're looking at the stars
The night has now gone
For this night has been long
After the blessing of light
There will be another bad war night.

Ximena Arnold (9)
Barnfields Primary School, Stafford

Autumn - Tanka

Brown shiny conkers
From the damp, wet, slippery branch
Autumn is here now
The leaves are bright and shiny
The animals get ready.

Ellie Rayner (9)
Barnfields Primary School, Stafford

Autumn - Tanka

It is autumn now
Hooray, hooray, leaves each day
Covering the ground
Squirrels getting food today
It is hibernation now.

Callum Aston (10)
Barnfields Primary School, Stafford

Evacuated

Here comes the train, down the track.
I wonder whether I'll come back.
I hear the mothers say goodbye
And all the children cry and cry.
We got on feeling very lonely
The train puffed on very slowly,
We picked up speed through the countryside
And still some children cried and cried.
Children clung onto their belongings very tight,
But some were just startled with fright.
We finally arrived there at last,
I wonder how soon this war will pass!

Sean Baker (10)
Barnfields Primary School, Stafford

Autumn - Tanka

Watch the colours change
In the autumn's awful rain.
Watch leaves fall from trees
As the soft leaves touch the ground.
Birds gather food for winter.

Harry Bowers (9)
Barnfields Primary School, Stafford

Autumn - Tanka

I was loving spring.
It had nature in the leaves.
It had red, green leaves.
I had seen bonfires burning.
Trees were getting blown over.

Samuel Howard (9)
Barnfields Primary School, Stafford

War

What can I see?
Many children sobbing violently,
Scared as babies who have just been born,
The driver with his head down, watching sadly,
The children carry gas masks round their necks.

What can I hear?
The sound of children sobbing louder and louder,
The driver waking the sleeping children,
Hundreds of children sobbing and sobbing,
Holding their luggage tighter than a person hanging from a cliff.

What can I feel?
I feel safer then a sleeping baby,
I feel heartbroken and speechless,
More afraid than a person standing in the front of a train,
On the train it feels terrifying.

Alex Baker (8)
Barnfields Primary School, Stafford

Being Evacuated

I'm on my own,
Alone at the railway station.
I'm in a lonely situation.
I see the bombs exploding
And air raid sirens echoing.
I can see the flames and fire.
My parents are my desire.
Then I hear the train coming,
It's time to leave my city.
I don't want to leave.
I climb onto the train.
My mum and dad are weeping.
I wave them goodbye.

Illqa Butt (9)
Barnfields Primary School, Stafford

Evacuation

What can you see?
I see people running to the shelters.
Lots of people with gas masks, ready for the gassy explosion.
German planes flying high in the sky.
Mothers and children sobbing as they have to separate.

What can you hear?
Guns being fired - deafening noises.
Bombs exploding all around.
Air raid sirens meaning more attacks.
Mothers and children sobbing as they have to say goodbye.

What can you feel?
I feel terrified, oh so terrified.
I feel hatred for the people of war.
I feel distraught in the colourless crowd.
Cold with fright as I have to go.

James Clayton (8)
Barnfields Primary School, Stafford

Evacuee

What can you see?
Smoke flying in the air.
Dust flying up and up.
Flaming, burning fires
And trains coming back and forth.

What can you hear?
Bombs exploding one by one.
The noise of the train.
Someone in pain.
The train blows its whistle.

How do you feel?
So terrified, but happy in a way.
Worried in case the train breaks down
But I don't want to say goodbye.
When I left I was angry.

Callum Carlisle (9)
Barnfields Primary School, Stafford

The Very Big War

What can I see?
Children with gas masks
The driver staring in tears
A lot of trains running along the track
Officers waving their flags.

What can I hear?
The train clattering along the track
The sound of people weeping
The air raid siren getting louder
The church bells ringing.

How do I feel?
I am completely terrified
I am heartbroken
I am annoyed
I am speechless and frightened to death.

Matthew Donoghue (8)
Barnfields Primary School, Stafford

Going Away

All around me bombs exploding,
People are dying, houses are broken,
Everything is horrible, especially leaving,
I hear the train pull into the station,
On the train it is silent, everybody is scared,
Off the train I get, the church bells are ringing,
Try to find a house to stay in, everything is quiet,
I feel happy but sad at the same time,
Everything is different, it feels really strange,
I meet my owner, I feel more settled,
But when war ends then I'll be back home.

Rebecca Clayton (9)
Barnfields Primary School, Stafford

Evacuees

The station made me feel as cold as ice,
Even though I'd had some hot rice.
I heard the mothers cry
As the children said bye-bye.
I went on a train at the station
To go to a scary destination,
As we went to the countryside
With my brother by my side.
As I saw the trees
With really green leaves
It looked like we'd left our station
As we reached our destination.
Our destination was such good fun
As we watched the hot sun.

Tauhir Edwards (10)
Barnfields Primary School, Stafford

The Evacuation

Sad driver watching the children board the train.
Weeping evacuees watching bright bombs like golden stars in the sky.
Parents crying because their children are leaving.
Officers organising the evacuees.

Mums crying and distraught,
Church bells ringing in my ear.
Chatting people talking to each other,
Army trucks going past.

I feel bad and distraught,
I feel sad as well.
I feel scared too,
I feel weak and weepy.

Jack Fidgett (8)
Barnfields Primary School, Stafford

Evacuation

This is what I hear . . .
Bombs exploding every night.
The sound of machine guns.
Trains screeching into the station.
Weeping people, saying goodbye.

This is what I see . . .
Planes soaring through the sky.
Billeting officers taking children to their destination.
Trains pulling into the station.
People preparing bomb shelters.

This is what I feel being an evacuee . . .
I feel terrified.
I feel shocked.
I feel lonely.
I feel nervous.

Matthew Firth (9)
Barnfields Primary School, Stafford

Stormy Day

Staring out the window
with nothing to play.
Watching the rain pour
on a horrible day.

The thunder booms loudly
and the sky is dull.
The lightning strikes down
like the horns of a bull.

Sitting there, still nothing to do.
In comes the teacher, Mrs Drew.
I sit down in my chair
and wish I were as furry as a bear.

Andrew Massey (10)
Barnfields Primary School, Stafford

I Am The School Bus

I'm not feeling very well,
After the big school bell.
The children are wearing me down,
Some days I just frown.
I'm growing very old,
You can see by the mould.
The windows are all rusty,
The seats are all musty.
I am the school bus!

Joel Lloyd (10)
Barnfields Primary School, Stafford

Being Evacuated

Being evacuated is very tense.
Standing there just hearing the rest.
Waiting for the train to come.
One by one that's how it's done.
Stopping and waiting in the dark night.
When you hear the exploding bombs.
Then you hear the weeping mums.
Hear the whistle blow on the train.
Off we go again.

Parminder Garcha (9)
Barnfields Primary School, Stafford

Evacuation

I was going away from home.
Soldiers were stamping, no one by me.
Boys were crying, girls were weeping.
No one was saying a word.
How long would this war go on for?
What would happen to England?
Would I be coming back again?

Sam Jeavons (9)
Barnfields Primary School, Stafford

An Evacuee

Terrified children lined up in a queue
Mothers filling up bottles or flasks with warm things like stew
A colourless bunch getting on the train
A big crowd of women weeping in the rain
If you want to know, this is what I feel
Nervous of who I am going to be with
Shocked to see how my mum wants me to live
Very doubtful with loads of sudden thoughts
The horrible feeling of being distraught.
I am an evacuee and this is what I hear
Bombs blowing up late at night
Soldiers shouting, 'Fight, fight, fight.'
Moaning Margaret wailing out
Mum keeps on saying, 'Don't ever doubt.'
Oh why is it hard to be an evacuee?
Oh why does it have to happen to me?

Simon Pearce (9)
Barnfields Primary School, Stafford

Evacuated

I was being evacuated
I really did hate it.
I was cold, worried and heartbroken
These were the words which were spoken.
'This country is at war with Germany'.
My mum was weeping
Others were sleeping,
As I heard the train
I really felt the pain.
I fell asleep on the way
When I woke up I thought it would be OK.

Joanna Paisley (9)
Barnfields Primary School, Stafford

Evacuation

What can you see?
A colourless crowd waiting.
Mothers running into shelters.
The train waiting for us to climb aboard.
Bright bombs exploding into the dark evening sky.

What can you hear?
Soldiers marching into war.
Air raid sirens ringing loudly like a police car right up close.
Train drivers ringing impatiently.
Bombs bashing frequently down town.

How do you feel?
Lonely, like a puppy that has been taken from its mother
And taken to a country abroad.
Angry with the Germans for making this war happen.
As terrified as a baby kangaroo rejected by her mother
And left on the main road.
Annoyed with myself because I've left my parents behind.
It's horrid to be so far from home in a place I've never been.

Sarah Taylor-Knight (8)
Barnfields Primary School, Stafford

World War II

Do you remember when you were cold?
Marching, shooting and growing old.

Bang, bang, bang! The sound of a gun.
Oh my God, I miss my son!

Sing a song in a trench.
Sitting on a frozen bench.

For 4 years, shooting Germans.
I wonder if we're savages or really humans.

Jordan Bailey (10)
Barnfields Primary School, Stafford

Being Evacuated

What can you see?
Many heartbroken mothers
People hurrying to shelters
A tired train driver sobbing while he waits
Children waiting to get on the train.

What can you hear?
Weeping mothers
Bombs exploding
Luggage rattling
Officers telling us to hurry up.

How do you feel?
Alone
Worried
Hated
Cold with fright.

Am I going to like this place?
Am I? Am I?

Chloe Wardle-Taylor (8)
Barnfields Primary School, Stafford

Candy Shop

I like sweets and lollies
And jelly dollies
Rhubarb and custard
But I hate mustard.

Jars of toffee
Dipped in coffee
I like choco mice
As they're half price.

That's the candy shop.

Jack Pedley (10)
Barnfields Primary School, Stafford

Evacuated

What can you see?
Weeping mothers sadly leaving their children
The fiery bombs exploding wherever they land
Gas masks to protect us from the poisonous gases
People running to shelters to stay safe.

What can you hear?
Air raid sirens telling you to go to the shelters
Screaming people running and never stopping
Crying mothers and children in the rain
Shouting mothers saying goodbye.

How do you feel?
Dreadful feelings drifting through the air
Heartbroken leaving our mums
Frightened that our mums will die
Lonely and alone without our mums.

Charlotte Watkinson (9)
Barnfields Primary School, Stafford

Maths

It's test day. Oh can't we play?
My brain's melting. Oh what a day!
Times tables, give me a power,
Six sixes, twelve twelves, only got an hour.

It's test day. Oh can't we play?
My brain's melting. Oh what a day!
Addition, subtraction and multiplication,
Kids doing maths all over the nation.

It's test day. Can't we play?
My brain's melting. Oh what a day!
Corrections, do it again,
Great, the clock's turned, half-past ten.

James Stokes (10)
Barnfields Primary School, Stafford

A Tribute To India

India is a lovely place.
You feel their hospitality.
If you have never been before you feel really scared.
You feel the sadness of men and women
Who suffer alone without any money.

You see lovely people wearing saris with lovely designs.
You see the beggars on the street.
People turning a blind eye to their situation.
You cannot get a word in edgeways
Because everyone is rushing and walking.

Busy streets full of motorcars and scooters.
You hear the sound of people shouting but mostly talking.
You hear people trying to get business.
It drives you mad with all that beeping and honking.

So I left with all these memories
Which will never die.
Part of me will always belong there.

Jasmin Mahil (10)
Barnfields Primary School, Stafford

My Bike

My bike is rusty
It's old and battered
It clanks and clunks
And the light is shattered.

The inner tube is bust
The seat is torn
My bike is battered
My bike is worn.

Matthew Miller (10)
Barnfields Primary School, Stafford

School Time

I get up ready for school today
I get dressed and put my pyjamas away.
I brush my teeth, I comb my hair
I go downstairs and sit on the chair.

I eat my breakfast, I clean my plate
My mum takes me to the school gate.
I go to the door, my friends say, 'Hello.'
I hang up my coat and put my bag down below.

I go to my classroom and sit at my table
I sit opposite my good friend Mabel.
I go to my tray and get out my literacy book
I do all my work then my teacher has a look.

Next it's playtime, we go out of the door
But the heavens open and it starts to pour.
We try to shelter under a tree
But then it stops at twenty to three.

We hurry along in the sharp breeze
We go inside so we don't freeze.
As the bell goes we go into the cloakroom
I say to my friends, 'Bye-bye, see you soon!'

Abbie Anslow (11)
Barnfields Primary School, Stafford

My Hamster Barney

Running round the cage at night
When I am asleep
Sometimes when I hold him
He tries to have a bite.

Running in the hamster wheel
I wonder what's the noise
I really need to buy him
Just a few more toys.

Sam Smith (10)
Barnfields Primary School, Stafford

Sport

Sport, sport is so fun
Tie those laces and off you run,
Exercise will keep you fit
Whether it's football, tennis, swimming or cricket.
Out in the park with your mates
Racing around on rollerskates
Hit the ball as hard as you can
Imagine for one moment you're Tim Henman.
Dive off the springboard into the pool
With style and grace, oh so cool.

Abbie Hodson (10)
Barnfields Primary School, Stafford

My Garden

See the little seed shooting through the brown soil.
The hot summer sun looking down at the ground.
See the bees buzzing around getting food from flowers.
See the rain splashing on the ground.
See the worm digging a hole.
I hear the birds twittering all around.
I hear insects buzzing.
I hear the laughter of children.

Saminda Sahota (10))
Barnfields Primary School, Stafford

Horses

H acking across the light fields of brown.
O ak trees, flowers, small creatures all around.
R acing over ditches, stumbling up hills.
S peeding up quickly as I pass all the mills
E njoying coming up the lane, my ride was very good
S oon I'll get back to the yard and clean off the mud.

Sophie Miles (11)
Barnfields Primary School, Stafford

Autumn

It's autumn time again,
The leaves are turning colours
Red, orange, green and brown
All kinds of autumn colours.

It's autumn time again,
Nights are getting dark
Curtains shut in a rush
Before it gets too dark.

It's autumn again
Conkers are falling down
Ready to be picked on the ground.

It's autumn again
The days are getting cold
The sun is put away
For an autumn day.

Chloe Richardson (10)
Barnfields Primary School, Stafford

Formula 1

Formula 1, what a sport,
It's really bad when your team gets nought.
Zooming past in the blink of an eye,
Great we won, give me a high five.
Flying round the track, two minutes a lap,
This is no time to have a nap.
I'm out of control, I'm going to crash,
This is the end, *bash, bash, bash!*
Alonso came first, Button came last,
I crashed into Coulthard whilst driving so fast.
Formula 1, what a sport,
It's really bad when your team gets nought.

Jonathon Matthews (10)
Barnfields Primary School, Stafford

Full Moon Happenings

Down on the beach on a full moon's evening
A lonely fairy sits there weaving
Until a monster gives her a fright
She spreads her wings wide in full flight.

Back on the beach on a full moon's evening
The monster's confused, he thinks of leaving
But he spots a stray dog that he thinks looks yummy
He wants to eat it in his tummy.

Down in the forest on a full moon's night
Witches and wizards are having a fight
Sparks are flying in the air
Witches give wizards a terrible scare.

Snuggling in my bed on a full moon's night
I dream of having X-ray sight
I don't see the fairy hovering in flight
I wonder what will happen on this magical night.

Anna Birtley (10)
Barnfields Primary School, Stafford

My Birthday

As I walk down the stairs I feel excited.
I go in the living room and there I see . . .
Lots of presents just for me.
And there is Mum and Dad waiting for me.
They say, 'Happy birthday,' to me.
I open my presents and there I see
An MP3 player waiting for me.
I had a key to open a diary to look and see
My uncle came round and he said,
'I've got a treat, I hope you enjoy this.'
I open the present and there I see, a teddy bumblebee.
We went to the Wacky Warehouse for some tea.
I had a lovely time and it was the best birthday ever.

Katie Bratton (11)
Barnfields Primary School, Stafford

A Cat's Hallowe'en

Hissing, spitting, catching mice,
Giving people a big fright.
Doing things that are not nice,
It's scary because . . . tonight's the night.

Running, chasing, nearly there,
Pounding like a humongous bear,
Catching mice with a big sharp bite,
It's scary because . . . tonight's the night.

Screeching, clawing, on the wall,
One of them is going to fall,
Jumping up into a full moon's light,
It's scary because . . . tonight's the night.

Itching, scratching, caught the fleas,
Now being chased by a hive of bees,
This cat's been taught for being mean,
It's scary because it's cat Hallowe'en.

Jessica Jarvis (10)
Barnfields Primary School, Stafford

The Weird Witch

One day, or night I cannot tell
I sat down near a wishing well.
Then a witch peeked out of the trees,
She jumped up and shouted, 'Wee!'
The witch looked evil but was very weird.
She stopped and looked at me with a horrid fright,
Maybe it was the shadow of me in the night.
I never knew a witch would be afraid of me,
Oh no, I've been turned into a giant honeybee.
Oh thank goodness, it was all a dream.

Sophie Watterson (10)
Barnfields Primary School, Stafford

Oh Cold Winter

So cold, as cold as icebergs,
No leaves on the trees
Just icy cold branches in the winter.

So cold, as cold as icebergs,
As people wrap up warm
For the chilly nights,
Frights in the winter.

So cold, as cold as icebergs,
As people get ready for Hallowe'en,
Whoo! in the winter.

So cold, as cold as icebergs,
As people start to put up decorations
For the great day
When Santa comes and gives children presents,
Oh cold, freezing, chilly winter.

Holly Tarr (10)
Barnfields Primary School, Stafford

Playground

The noise of children playing here.
The roar of children blowing into my ear.
Clapping hands and chattering teeth.
It makes me think that I am a deer.

Cold winds blowing in my face.
The playground is a muddy place.
It feels as though you sink to the ground
But it's you not making a sound.

Here I am in the playground not making a sound.
Here's the bug that creeps around.
It makes me feel
Like I am lying on the ground.

Emma Taylor (10)
Barnfields Primary School, Stafford

Destruction Derby

Crashing, bashing as the cars collide
The roar of an engine like a lion fighting for its pride.

The cars flick dust like the sand on a beach
The people all clap as the cars make a screech.

The alloys fly off into the crowd
The lion has died and fallen to the ground.

They race around like lion cubs wanting to play
Race is over and the cars go away.

Jarred Raybould (10)
Barnfields Primary School, Stafford

Motocross

Scramblers doing jumps,
Going over all the bumps.
Doing tricks in the air
Some they do for a dare.

When they do a Superman
All the children laughed and ran.
All the dust flying around
While you hear the engine sound.

Jack Roestenburg (11)
Barnfields Primary School, Stafford

Autumn - Tanka

Frosty, cold, damp world,
The soggy, coloured leaves fall.
Crane flies come and go,
Prickly hedgehogs hibernate,
Shiny conkers on wet grass.

Emily Banks (9)
Barnfields Primary School, Stafford

My Dream

When you all are fast asleep
You might hear me gently weep.
My fists are clenched as tight as tight
I hug my pillow all through the night
But eventually I must have slept
And this dream it was the best
It wasn't like the rest
I dreamt I was a fairy
With beautiful fluttering wings
I fluttered around the candy tree and heard the bluebirds sing
I fought with all the pirates and left them quivering in their boots
I even left old Captain Hook screaming with a hoot
So here I am in my bed
These beautiful images in my head
So here I am in my bed
This beautiful image in my head
Just fast asleep in my bed.

Charlotte Connolly (10)
Barnfields Primary School, Stafford

Crashing, Bashing!

Crashing cars, crashing cars.
Crash, crash, crush, crush! go the cars.
Crashing cars, crashing cars.
Keep on crashing,
All day long.

Bang, bang, bang!
Ching, ching, chang!
Goes the Chinese racer.

Boom, boom, boom!
Goes the old rusty car,
As the beer goes off the bar.

Adam Greer (10)
Barnfields Primary School, Stafford

The Survival

Hednesford Raceway, Hednesford Raceway,
My favourite place to stay
As the bangers flip away
To go and get their prey.

Hednesford Raceway, Hednesford Raceway,
The coaches come today
On the track they burn away
On the twenty-second of May.

Hednesford Raceway, Hednesford Raceway,
The hot rods come today
But what a shame
It's reached the end of the day.

Andrew Franklin (11)
Barnfields Primary School, Stafford

Autumn - Tanka

Shiny brown conkers
Lying on dew-covered grass
Mist in frosty air
Amber, gold, red and dark brown
Are the colours of the leaves.

Freya Cleasby (9)
Barnfields Primary School, Stafford

Autumn - Tanka

I saw blood-red leaves.
Raindrops falling from the skies.
The trees ripe with fruit.
The conkers are falling now.
The autumn becomes winter.

Matthew Lovatt (9)
Barnfields Primary School, Stafford

Autumn - Tanka

The season is here
Where animals hibernate
Birds gather berries
Squirrels retrieve nuts and fruit
Must mean autumn has arrived.

Oliver Stanlake (9)
Barnfields Primary School, Stafford

Autumn - Tanka

People step on leaves
As they fall from the brown trees
From the big wide wood,
Suddenly a squirrel hides,
Before a big red fox comes.

Megan Challinor (10)
Barnfields Primary School, Stafford

Autumn - Tanka

Autumn time is here
All the leaves fall off the trees
Autumn time is here
The hedgehogs begin to hide
All the year is growing old.

Sammy Cooper (9)
Barnfields Primary School, Stafford

Autumn - Tanka

I saw coloured leaves
I saw a bonfire burning
Trees with yellow leaves
Autumn has come and is great
Lots of coloured leaves and red.

Rupert Thomas
Barnfields Primary School, Stafford

Autumn - Tanka

I'm getting ready
For a special autumn day.
Conkers falling down,
We are singing round the fire
Enjoying our autumn day.

Megan Jenks (9)
Barnfields Primary School, Stafford

Autumn - Tanka

Autumn is here now
Watch the leaves come falling down
All red and crispy
Falling gently on the ground
Squirrels are gathering food.

David Edge (9)
Barnfields Primary School, Stafford

Autumn - Tanka

It's autumn again.
The leaves turning brownish red.
The conkers falling,
The squirrels gathering nuts,
It is autumn time again.

Daniel Clarke (9)
Barnfields Primary School, Stafford

Autumn - Tanka

Shiny brown conkers
For the children to play with
But if one should break
You could always get some more.
Conkers are ever so fun.

David Anderson (9)
Barnfields Primary School, Stafford

Autumn - Tanka

When the leaves fall down
To the ground and blow away
And hit the ground soft
Conkers hit the ground quite hard,
Then they get picked by people.

Joshua Key (9)
Barnfields Primary School, Stafford

Autumn - Tanka

Leaves shoot to the ground.
Soft berries hang, yet no sound.
Roast chestnuts eaten.
Outside your house, fog like steam.
The conker shell opens up.

Lois Calder (9)
Barnfields Primary School, Stafford

Autumn - Tanka

Twirling from the trees
Leaves are coloured golden-brown
Flowers curl up dead
Squirrels break conker cases
Birds are gathering for flight.

Bethany Lee (9)
Barnfields Primary School, Stafford

Autumn - Tanka

I am a conker
I have fallen off a tree
Wrapped up in my shell
Now it's time for me to see
And to feel the damp wind blow.

Lauren Hough (9)
Barnfields Primary School, Stafford

Autumn - Tanka

Feeling the soft breeze
It's amazing how it seems
Conkers are falling
Leaves are dancing all around
Can you hear the lovely sounds?

Antonia Bailey (10)
Barnfields Primary School, Stafford

Autumn - Tanka

When the birds migrate,
Conkers fall from the trees hard,
Squirrels eating nuts,
Leaves softly drop from the trees,
Leaves change colours quietly.

Jack Smith (9)
Barnfields Primary School, Stafford

Autumn - Tanka

When the leaves fall down
Their colours, yellow and red.
Trees with a brown stalk.
Conkers like they've been polished.
People pick the conkers too.

Clare Lester (9)
Barnfields Primary School, Stafford

Autumn - Tanka

Autumn time is here,
Bright red leaves with gold shading,
Brown sparkling conkers,
Squirrels, hedgehogs hibernate,
The fireworks make a loud *bang!*

Jake Triggs (9)
Barnfields Primary School, Stafford

Autumn

Conkers round and shiny brown.
Some are white and some are brown.
Leaves fall from the tree.
Some leaves are red and some are yellow.
Animals hibernate now.

Eleanor Coates (9)
Barnfields Primary School, Stafford

Autumn

Conkers lie waiting.
Leaves land on the ground.
Birds fly round.
The clocks start to chime
Because it is autumn time.

Connor Smith (9)
Barnfields Primary School, Stafford

My Shadow

There's a black, bold, scary someone,
everything I do it has done.

It's on my left then on my right,
it's there in the day but not at night.

It's on the floor or on the wall,
it's very big or really small.

It's always there when I'm alone,
it doesn't seem to have one bone.

It actually always copies me,
it has no features you will see.

I reckon it's my special friend,
but it drives me round the bend.

I finally realise what it is,
it's my *shadow!*

Alice Cotton (9)
Barrow CE Primary School, Broseley

Is This A Real Snake?

My best friend is a snake
and his name is Silly Drake,
when I see him he is small
even though he is quite tall.

My snake friend is a cobra
sometimes through he is sober
he is also very long
and so is his enormous tongue.

My snake, Silly Drake,
loves to swim in a lake,
when he spits, it is Coke
sometimes though he will choke.

Joseph Anderson (10)
Barrow CE Primary School, Broseley

Remembering

We will remember
those who were lost,
things are now normal,
but it came at a cost.

One minute's silence
and lots of tears,
some 'brainwashed' Muslims
brought out our fears.

May their souls rest in Heaven
and never be sad,
they won't go to Hell
as they did nothing bad.

May we forgive those
whose minds went astray,
but now it's all over
and it's a new day.

James Challenor (10)
Barrow CE Primary School, Broseley

Trees Of Australia

In Australia there are many trees,
On the island surrounded by seas.

Mangroves, messy, meandering and manky,
Small, thin, not at all lanky.

Deadly spiders in the bark,
Never go near them in the dark!

Crocodiles curl cautiously round,
Making sure they don't make a sound.

The mangroves look extremely haunted,
But even so I'm not very daunted!

Mangroves can be found all round,
Especially in the boggy ground.

Nicole Wellsford (10)
Barrow CE Primary School, Broseley

Nothing But Winter

Winter, winter with all the ice,
As cold as little frozen mice,

Winter storms blow in.

Slippery, sliding, slithery snow,
Avalanches down, cold but slow,

Winter storms blow in.

Everything covered, nothing but white,
Such a beautiful wonderful sight,

Winter storms blow in.

The owls snuggle up as the night blows on,
Wolves scarcely howling as the midnight shone,

Winter storms blow in.

Wonderful winter comes each year,
Beautiful winter is always here,

Winter storms blow in.

Laura-Beth Bowen (10)
Barrow CE Primary School, Broseley

The Frogs

Hip-hop, hip-hop, hip-hop,
splash in the water with a *plop*.

A frog needs a tasty snack,
buzzing around small and black.

Some are small and some are tall,
some are lean like a ball.

They come in several different types,
some have armour just like knights.

Some are really horrible and nasty,
and you'll end up a squashed pasty.

Some greet you nicely and well
some give off a horrible smell.

Mothers lay the tiny frogspawn,
hooray the babies are finally born.

Hip-hop, hip-hop, hip-hop,
splashing in the water with a *plop*.

Jordan Clarke (10)
Barrow CE Primary School, Broseley

A Victorian Mine

E mergency, emergency, an explosion went off,
X -ray the whole place, I think somebody is trapped,
P eople blown up, I ran to the nearest person,
L et the whole town know,
O ver there I last saw a hand,
S ave them, save them,
I call with my loudest voice,
O n the other side I can hear a weak voice,
N obody can reach the cries.

Heather Simcock (8)
Clive CE Primary School, Shrewsbury

Cart

C oal getting shoved in a cart
A fter a while you feel your heart
R acing and pounding
T errified people listen to a sound.

I n a terrible earthquake which shook the ground
N ever-ending mist four miles around

A massive silence in the mine

M illions of people listen for a sign
I f people were hurt
N ever happy shouts
E nded by a cry of doubt.

Rory Bothwell (10)
Clive CE Primary School, Shrewsbury

The Mine

Deep underground people rush through
The damp gooey mine with dripping walls
Tunnels really dark and mysterious
Hearing screams and coal falling from the roof
Big explosions, history screams.

Robert Hughes (8)
Clive CE Primary School, Shrewsbury

The Death Mine

Down, down deep in the mine,
Sunless and funless people dying and crying,
Hacking and whacking the slimy black walls.
I truly think this is a death cave,
The cave of the Devil.

Henry Walker (9)
Clive CE Primary School, Shrewsbury

The Mine

T he clammy roofs are very low and my job is to walk the horse
H orses' hooves fill the air as the horse staggers through the mine
E choes fill the air as workers work underneath their overhangs
M ining with explosives can lead to danger zones where gas comes
through
I n the mine there is a boy called Billy that opens and shuts the
door for me and the horse
N ear the exit I walk as the blinding sun hits my eyes. It's very
terrifying in a mine.
E xiting the mine at the end of the day, I only get a few pennies a day.

Nina M Andersen Smith (10)
Clive CE Primary School, Shrewsbury

Explosion

E   ntering the entrance
E X citing explosion
P   ounding pain
L   ost and labouring
O   beying orders
S   queezing suffocation
Fl I ckering fuses
O   bjects flying
N   ear screams.

John O'Neill (8)
Clive CE Primary School, Shrewsbury

Mine

M urky and dark
I n the mine it felt like back in time
N asty and dark down the terrifying mine
E xplosions blast through the solid rock.

Ryan Wall (10)
Clive CE Primary School, Shrewsbury

The Mine

As I entered the sunless and damp mine
I heard the clinging and clanging . . .
Of pickaxes coming closer and closer
The miners were shouting,
'Where's the rope lighter?'
I realised I was that person
I pelted down the passageways
Cutting my arms on the rocks
Lighting a candle I ran to the rope
I grabbed the horse and led her quickly
Horrid visions of people dead
Came into my head
The sound of injured people
Screaming for help rang through the mine
I shed tears as I ran for shelter.

Jack Morgan (8)
Clive CE Primary School, Shrewsbury

Down The Mine

It was as black as the darkest night,
All I could see was the flicker . . .
Of candlelight,
The sound of pickaxes . . .
Hitting the coal.

My heart pounded as I heard,
The explosion,
The ground shook with anger,
All I could hear was the sound of
The miners' pounding feet.

Bethany Greene (10)
Clive CE Primary School, Shrewsbury

The Mine

I walked into a sunless hole,
No light but sound as quiet as a mouse.
As I stepped closer sound grew louder,
The black was growing lighter
Until it was everywhere,
Clinking was coming from all the sides,
As men thumped at the ghastly walls.
Carts screeched round the corners
Full of the darkest coal
A great blast came from the tunnel,
Dusty men dashed from the mine.
Crying to get out
I ran fast to higher ground
I looked back at the once black mine,
Now ablaze with many candles.
The cry of the unlucky was faint,
But the words were heard
And remembered by the ones that were lucky that day.

Matthew Simcock (11)
Clive CE Primary School, Shrewsbury

The Mine

T he mine is sunless all day through
H eaving the coal is risky too
E xplosives were set, all ready and wet

M isty and damp is the mine
I n a damp wet spot it goes all quiet and cold
N ot many survivors saved the mine
E xcitement reaches when they end the mine.

Thomas Hughes (10)
Clive CE Primary School, Shrewsbury

Working In The Mine

W orking
O n the ladder
R isking
K eeping safe
I nsecure
N o light
G loomy

I gnite
N oises

T hreatening
H orses
E nliven

M oisture
I nside the mine
N asty explosives
E ndangerment.

Samantha Turner (9)
Clive CE Primary School, Shrewsbury

The Mine

T he mine was dark and terrifying
H orrible and dusky
E xplosives banging down the mine, knocking the coal

M urky and dull down the mine
I nside the mine were creepy noises
N asty, nifty smells
E xcellent, exciting darkness.

Prentice Hazell (8)
Clive CE Primary School, Shrewsbury

The Mine

In the mine as dark as night,
It's hard to see when there's no light.
The flickering of the candle flame,
My horse was beginning to get very lame.
I heard the fizzing of dynamite
And then a big enormous flash of light.
I wished and wished to be at home,
To never be again alone.

Emily Jennings (9)
Clive CE Primary School, Shrewsbury

The Mine

Dark and gloomy
The mine is scary, you
Will always have a pickaxe
No time to relax. Some mines
Are soggy, you will get caught by
The Doggy. Shovelling the
Coal, digging like a mole
Eating is rare, you
Will always
Get a
Scare.

Gus Langford (8)
Clive CE Primary School, Shrewsbury

Mine Of The Devil

M oney is not enough,
I slave and will probably die for this mine,
N o one will survive this death cave,
E veryone dies, this is the mine of the Devil.

James Walker (9)
Clive CE Primary School, Shrewsbury

Victorian Mines

Miners working down the mines
Hacking coal from the slimy black walls
Sparking, fizzling dynamite
People dashing and blundering in the darkness of night
The enormous explosion made the cart overturn
And the horse galloped off down the dark, dripping tunnel
Total confusion
Deep underground
A Victorian mine.

Helena Wall (8)
Clive CE Primary School, Shrewsbury

A Victorian Mine

Down, down, down deep in the mine,
A gravely crunch all over the ground,
Horses pulling carts through narrow passageways,
The smell of dirt and dust,
My shirt is thin
And my spine is shivering,
Shivering cold,
Shivering cold.

Megan Greene (8)
Clive CE Primary School, Shrewsbury

Workers

W orking workers
O beying orders
R ats climb cliffs
K eeping safe
E verything is dangerous down a mine
R isking lives every day
S uffering miners.

Max Withey (8)
Clive CE Primary School, Shrewsbury

A Victorian Mine

The pitch-black mine, so damp and dripping,
The miners' bones so aching.
The heavy wooden props just managing,
The flickering candles just giving enough light.

The explosives about to go off,
The miners just about fast enough.
Though some are not.
The great bang going off,
The coal falling heavily and fast.
The muffled yelling just heard from the sound of the buried,
The dust all settling over the heavy rubble.

Emma Black (9)
Clive CE Primary School, Shrewsbury

A Victorian Mine

Down, down deep in the mine
I open the door
Only a flicker of candlelight to see
All I can hear are cries
And crumbling coal from the ghostly distance
Mysterious drips from coal walls
I hear an explosion, my heart pounds
I feel scared and frightened
I know someone will be hurt.

Laura Grantham (8)
Clive CE Primary School, Shrewsbury

Autumn

The man's skin is as rough as sandpaper
His wrinkles are like prunes, dried up
His tears float down to the ground on his feet
His mouth, a hole, is big and wide
His bendy arms wave bare in the fresh air
His big brown feet stick to the floor
Long bony fingers rustle in the wind
His colourful highlights shine in the sun.

Jodie Fisher & Holly Kettlewell (10)
Crescent School, Rugby

Autumn Trees

The tree gets old and loses his hair,
The tree has highlights every autumn,
The hands are waving high in the wind,
The trunk is the strong spine of the body,
The sap goes around the tree's body
Pumped through the veins to the fingertips,
The dark grey skin is scabbed all over,
The branches are going to bed, zzzzz.

Fabia Carney (10)
Crescent School, Rugby

Autumn

The feet are firm in the ground,
The fingers of the tree are bare,
The small toes are in the ground,
The tree is getting bald and old,
The scabs are rough and bumpy,
The tree has highlights every year.

James Leach (10)
Crescent School, Rugby

A Cold And Windy Autumn

The hands are waving as cold as an iceberg
Old man losing his hair, becoming bald
Grandma's hair having highlights as brown as possible
The fingers are wriggling on the cold day
The wild Mexican wave with all different colours
The old men with all rough and bumpy skin
The toes are frozen as cold as can be, going hard
The eyes are staring upon the creatures
The arms are resting with pretty beautiful birdies
An old, old man having his hair shaved off.

Lucy Powell (10)
Crescent School, Rugby

Autumn

Changes colour from green to brown,
Has hair brightly dyed in autumn.
Loses hair in autumn to grow it back in spring.
No more hearing the birds singing.
Dropping conkers, leaves and pine cones.
They sell fruit, apples and pears are very sweet,
Juicy and ready for us to gather and eat.
As they calmly wave in the breeze,
They will whisper and dance as well.
The streets are filled with molten hair,
That's the sign that autumn is there.

Gwen Edmunds (11)
Crescent School, Rugby

The Autumn Human Tree

I am talking to others,
Dancing as I wave my arms
And fingers round my head
In the cooling autumn breeze.
Skin peeling from my body
And I am dying my hair
Orange, gold, yellow and red
Before I become bald.
My feet are stuck in the ground
I am feeding through my feet.

Johanna Tooze (10)
Crescent School, Rugby

An Autumn Tree's Story

Getting ready to go to sleep.
Dandruff falling from my head.
I take the clothes off my body
And my hair drops off my head.
I let go of my small babies.
My hands wave solemnly goodbye.
The flesh comes off my skeleton.
My feet are stuck in the earth.

Qasim Mian (10)
Crescent School, Rugby

Autumn Term

The trees' feet stand firm in the ground
Their long skinny arms waving to you.
The hair's falling off the old man
And the girls are dying their hair orange
Hoping it will turn back next year.

Nancy Pomfrett (10)
Crescent School, Rugby

The Mysterious Tree

The old man is walking back home,
He discovers his house is covered in golden leaves.
The old man goes inside, everything is golden and brown.
Suddenly his feet get stuck in the ground, he is a tree
His hair turned into brown leaves.
There are branches coming out from his old body,
His hair starts to fall off faster and faster.
He can't move his spine, it's as solid as a piece of brick.
He has no feet, they are muddy roots.
Suddenly the wind comes through into his house,
Branches fall off him, he is an autumn tree.

Joanna Hall (10)
Crescent School, Rugby

Autumn

The feet are firmly stuck in the mud
Old man losing hair and becoming bald
The hands are waving in the strong wind
The bark is coming off like old scabs
The old women with old bumpy skin
The hair is whispering quietly
The toes are moving slowly in mud
The hair has brown highlights in the sun
The body is moving from side to side
The hair is crinkling up and dying.

Huw Phillips (10)
Crescent School, Rugby

Autumn

I am walking down the cobbled path
Kicking the leaves in my way
Suddenly I see this weird thing
Doing hilarious things
Waving hands in the damp rainy air
Calling for help constantly
'My feet are stuck to the mud,' he cries
'And my hair is turning gold.'
'What can I do for you?' I proclaim.
'There's nothing much you can do,
Summer has gone and autumn is back.'

Sebastian Coulthread (10)
Crescent School, Rugby

The Human Tree

An old man's hair falling out.
Hands waving in the wind.
Fingers in the wind look like they're playing the piano.

The leaves whisper in the wind.
Its skin is hard and rough.
It is stretched up to the sky with its super, large, long arms.

It is dancing in a gale
Hands waving in the wind.
Very sticky blood oozes out of my big fat body.

Annalise Thornhill (10)
Crescent School, Rugby

Autumn

The ageing man is losing hair,
The man's skin is peeling skin,
The arms are swaying in the wind,
His feet are glued in the ground,
The man's hair is changing colour,
The man has lots of rough skin,
The man has broken a frail bone.

Joseph Chappell (10)
Crescent School, Rugby

Autumn

Lovely, shiny, golden highlights
Golden hair gone, now bald and old
Dirty, old and bald burnt head
Old, dirty, wrinkled, dull face
Dirty and bony waving hands
Very white bony skeleton
Quite long, lazy, bony legs
Big tired feet stuck in mud
Surrounded by golden hair.

Libby Wilson (11) & Harriet Pigott (10)
Crescent School, Rugby

Dogs Of The Week

Monday's dog is stupid and dumb
Tuesday's dog is stealing Dad's rum
Wednesday's dog is drinking beer
Thursday's dog has killed a deer
Friday's dog has eaten a fox
Saturday's dog is as strong as an ox
And the dog that is born on the seventh day
Is the toughest dog on the streets of LA.

Edward Bennett (8)
Flash Ley Primary School, Stafford

Dogs Of The Week

Monday's dog is big and hairy
Tuesday's dog is Scary Mary
Wednesday's dog drinks giant whisky
Thursday's dog is very frisky
Friday's dog eats all sorts of stuff
Saturday's dog leaps off the roof
And the dog that was born on the seventh day
Always likes to slay the hay.

Joshua Whitmore (8)
Flash Ley Primary School, Stafford

Dogs Of The Week

Monday's dog is a scruffy dog
Tuesday's dog is as stupid as a frog
Wednesday's dog feels like a dove
Thursday's dog smells like Duff
Friday's dog is big and fat
Saturday's dog always lies on the mat
And the dog that was born on the seventh day
Likes to roll in the hay.

Joshua Wingate (9)
Flash Ley Primary School, Stafford

Dogs Of The Week

Monday's dog smells of beer
Tuesday's dog runs like a deer
Wednesday's dog is as fat as a pig
Thursday's dog likes playing tig
Friday's dog is as big as a bear
Saturday's dog is as small as a pear
And the dog that is born on the seventh day
Always wants to play, play, play.

James Ostle (8)
Flash Ley Primary School, Stafford

Dogs Of The Week

Monday's dog is fat and smelly
Tuesday's dog is chewing a wellie
Wednesday's dog is chasing a fly
Thursday's dog just wants to die
Friday's dog steals Dad's money
Saturday's dog eats the honey
And the dog that was born on the seventh day
Goes in the canal for a holiday.

Daniel Evans (8)
Flash Ley Primary School, Stafford

Dogs Of The Week

Monday's dog tries to fly
Tuesday's dog wants to die
Wednesday's dog bites Dad's bum
Thursday's dog licks his gum
Friday's dog smells like old socks
Saturday's dog always looks at the clock
And the dog that was born on the seventh day
His favourite food is egg and hay.

Adam Campbell (9)
Flash Ley Primary School, Stafford

Dogs Of The Week

Monday's dog has got some fleas
Tuesday's dog is begging on his knees
Wednesday's dog is fat and smelly
Thursday's dog puts onions in his belly
Friday's dog has got a girlfriend called Honey
Saturday's dog is mugging Dad for money
And the dog that was born on the seventh day
Has gone out with his girlfriend all day, all day.

Katie Bailey (9)
Flash Ley Primary School, Stafford

Monday's Dog

Monday's dog rounds up the herds
Tuesday's dog feeds the birds
Wednesday's dog is called Peter
Thursday's dog is such an eater
Friday's dog rips up paper
Saturday's dog is a scraper
And the dog that was born on the seventh day
Is always told to stay away.

Rachel Sharp (8)
Flash Ley Primary School, Stafford

Dogs Of The Week

Monday's dog fell in some dung
Tuesday's dog goes *'Katchung'*
Wednesday's dog uses the loo
Thursday's dog has the flu
Friday's dog takes pills
Saturday's dog always kills
And the dog that was born on the seventh day
Is the one who flies away.

Darcie-May Luckman (9)
Flash Ley Primary School, Stafford

Dogs Of The Week

Monday's dog will trip you up
Tuesday's dog always has a pup
Wednesday's dog is always yapping
Thursday's dog is always snapping
Friday's dog is always gay
Saturday's dog is waiting for May
And the dog that was born on the seventh day
Will always run away.

Victoria Boulton (9)
Flash Ley Primary School, Stafford

Dogs Of The Week

Monday's dog is round and fat
Tuesday's dog sits on a mat
Wednesday's dog catches the mouse
Thursday's dog is not very nice
Friday's dog likes a pot
Saturday's dog has a nasty spot
And the dog that was born on the seventh day
Is so spotty and gay.

Courtney Heathcote (9)
Flash Ley Primary School, Stafford

Dogs Of The Week

Monday's dog is really tough
Tuesday's dog is really rough
Wednesday's dog has a runny nose
Thursday's dog likes to pose
Friday's dog is really fluffy
Saturday's dog is not too lucky
And the dog that was born on the seventh day
He goes to the shop and shouts, 'Hooray!'

Alisha Tomson (8)
Flash Ley Primary School, Stafford

Dogs Of The Week

Monday's dog is tired and scruffy
Tuesday's dog is pretty and fluffy
Wednesday's dog acts like Cinderella
Thursday's dog is a big bad fella
Friday's dog has a girlfriend called Ella
Saturday's dog likes to drink a beer that's Stella
And the dog that was born on the seventh day
Is naughty and cruel and is told to stay.

Chelsea Reece (9)
Flash Ley Primary School, Stafford

Dogs Of The Week

Monday's dog is very fat
Tuesday's dog wants a cat
Wednesday's dog has a bag
Thursday's dog has a tail that wags
Friday's dog looks bad
Saturday's dog isn't so glad
And the dog that was born on the seventh day
Eats all the horses in the hay.

Chloe Denniss (8)
Flash Ley Primary School, Stafford

Dogs Of The Week

Monday's dog is fat in the belly
Tuesday's dog digs for wellies
Wednesday's dog has floppy ears
Thursday's dog is full of tears
Friday's dog has a spotty belly
Saturday's dog is smelly
And the dog that was born on the seventh day
Likes to eat jelly for half the day.

Tammy Tomlinson (8)
Flash Ley Primary School, Stafford

Dogs Of The Week

Monday's dog is big and smelly
Tuesday's dog always watches the telly
Wednesday's dog jumps and plays
Thursday's dog runs away
Friday's dog smells like old socks
Saturday's dog has curly locks
And the dog that was born on the seventh day
Will go to the kennels for a holiday.

Treasure Edwards (8)
Flash Ley Primary School, Stafford

The Magic Box
(Based on 'Magic Box' by Kit Wright)

I will put in the box . . .

The sound of a
dolphin splashing
in the waves.

The feel of the
fluffiest chick.

I will put in the box . . .

Tinkerbell on top
of a Disney castle.

My box is fashioned
from ice with the
moon and stars on
the lid.

Its hinges are made
from a
whale's mouth.

Rebecca Plant (7)
Flash Ley Primary School, Stafford

Dogs Of The Week

Monday's dog is fat and smelly
Tuesday's dog has got a girlfriend called Kelly
Wednesday's dog chases the cat
Thursday's dog is just too fat
Friday's dog loves to play
Saturday's dog hides in the hay
And the dog that was born on the seventh day
Goes on holiday.

Aysha Longdon (8)
Flash Ley Primary School, Stafford

The Magic Box

(Based on 'Magic Box' by Kit Wright)

I will put in the box . . .

The howl of a black
hairy hound.

The feel of a foamy
fearsome sea.

The bellow of a
gorilla beating its
gigantic chest.

I will put in the box . . .

The scratchy scales
of a slithering slim snake.

I would like to taste
a tremendous pear.

My box is fashioned
from flames from
the sun and craters
from the moon

With shooting stars
on the lid and
foreign languages in
the corners.

Its hinges are made
from frogs'
webbed feet.

Caitlin Foster (7)
Flash Ley Primary School, Stafford

The Magic Box

(Based on 'Magic Box' by Kit Wright)

I will put in my box . . .

The feel of a small,
smooth, slimy slug.

I will put in my box . . .

The feel of my dog's
furry hair.

The sound of an elephant
stamping its foot.

My box is fashioned
from black coal and seeds
with spider legs on the corners.

On the hinges
there are frogs' legs.

Lauren Robb (7)
Flash Ley Primary School, Stafford

The Magic Box

(Based on 'Magic Box' by Kit Wright)

I will put in the box . . .

The sound of a seal splashing in the sea,
The feel of a snail's shiny shell.

I will put in the box . . .

The sight of a crab
Moving side to side
The taste of chicken noodles.

My box is fashioned from
Fireworks and a sparkling crown
With shiny diamonds.

Kyle Parsons (7)
Flash Ley Primary School, Stafford

The Magic Box

(Based on 'Magic Box' by Kit Wright)

I will put in the box . . .

The sound of a dolphin splashing in the waves,
The feel of the fluffiest chick.

I will put in the box . . .

A whale swimming in the deep water of the sea.
I like to taste chocolate ice cream.

My box is fashioned from ice
With moon and stars on the lid.
Its hinges are made from a whale's mouth.

Elliot Jones (8)
Flash Ley Primary School, Stafford

The Magic Box

(Based on 'Magic Box' by Kit Wright)

I will put in the box . . .

A sound of a gorilla
beating his chest.

A feel of a football stud
on a golden boot.

I will put in the box . . .

A jellyfish floating away
in the deep, blue ocean.

The taste of an octopus
swimming away in a crashed ship.

My box is fashioned
from a horseshoe and gold corn
with ice cream on the lid.

Sarah Corbett (7)
Flash Ley Primary School, Stafford

The Magic Box

(Based on 'Magic Box' by Kit Wright)

My box is fashioned from
Rainbows' beams and flower petals.

The lid is covered in wizards' wands,
Frogs and hedgehogs,
Its hinges are made from hot dragon tails.

Sam McNamara (7)
Flash Ley Primary School, Stafford

Fireworks

Flashing when they got as high as they could,
I saw crimson lights in the sky,
Racing in the heavens.
Ear-splitting.
Whistling upwards.
Orange and blue
Hissing and exploding
Catherine wheels.
Round Roman candles like a fountain,
Kindled so bright.
Spectacular November display.

Timothy Ratcliffe (11)
Flash Ley Primary School, Stafford

The River Of Life

I was a bright babbling spring dancing down the mountains,
As I got older I splashed down a waterfall or two,
Jumping and leaping over rocks.
When I got older I got tired and quiet,
At last I ended up in the sea.
I will live forever.

Jessica Wheatley (10)
Flash Ley Primary School, Stafford

Dog Talk

Pebbles and shells
Water down wells
Churches and bells
Your dog smells.

Sand and waves
Bats and caves
Rants and raves
My dog behaves.

Beetles and slugs
Fleas and rugs
Kisses and hugs
Your dog's got bugs.

Keys and locks
Feet and socks
Eagles and hawks
My dog talks!

Anna Boulton (10)
Flash Ley Primary School, Stafford

The River Of Life

I am a babbling brook starting off on my journey,
I am following the river and skipping down the mountain,
Splattering and splashing and running on the rocks.
Now I am dawdling and quiet and still as I flow into the sea.

Robert Kempson (10)
Flash Ley Primary School, Stafford

The River Of Life

I am skipping down the mountain,
Screaming down the waterfall.
I am spraying round the river,
Slowly travelling into the sea.

Mark Moffat (9)
Flash Ley Primary School, Stafford

The Magic Box
(Based on 'Magic Box' by Kit Wright)

I will put in the box . . .

The howl of a black hairy hound,
The feel of a foamy fearsome sea,
The bellow of a gorilla beating its gigantic chest.

I will put in the box . . .

The scales of a slim slithering snake,
I would like to taste the juiciest tremendous pear.

My box is fashioned from flames from the sun
And craters from the moon,
With shooting stars on the lid
And foreign languages in the corners.

Its hinges are made from frogs' webbed feet.

David Li (7)
Flash Ley Primary School, Stafford

My Simile Poem - Wind

It was a bright early morning,
the wind was throwing leaves around
like a baby in a tantrum.
You could hear the wind thumping
the branches of the gnarled trees,
like a bully in the playground.

Adrian Wood (11)
Flash Ley Primary School, Stafford

My Simile Poem - Monster

Its head is like a serpent,
Its body is like a dragon ready to attack,
Its claws are like sharp razors,
Its teeth are like a broken bottle, sharp and bloody.

Joseph Bush (10)
Flash Ley Primary School, Stafford

Breathless

Dive in the pool
Cold water
Swim fast
Panting quickly
Bad stitch
Splashing water
Goggles leaking
Costume rubbing
Need a drink
Must carry on
Very tired
Legs aching
Catch up with someone
Kicking fast
Need to stop
Getting hot
Finally finished.

Alice Holmes (10)
Flash Ley Primary School, Stafford

Fireworks

Fireworks whispering in fountains of colours
As they shoot up into the jet-black sky.
Pink, crimson, sapphire, yellow,
Whines and screeches in the jet-black wind.
Dancing flames spitting and swirling everywhere you go.

Cally Sadler (10)
Flash Ley Primary School, Stafford

Breathless

Light sky
Green grass
Warm air
My heart
Lots of trees
Swaying side to side
The race started
Ready, steady, go
I run, I run
I run as fast as
I can
I am nearly there
My heart is pounding
My legs are aching
People cheering me on
I have, I've won
Hip hip hooray!
'First place
Goes to
Julie Philips.'

Julie Phillips (10)
Flash Ley Primary School, Stafford

My Simile Poem - Snowflakes

Snowflakes slowly falling down.
Feel like feathers as they touch your face
Like a long blanket covering everything.
Six-sided snowflakes in all shapes and sizes.

Kelcie Oakley (10)
Flash Ley Primary School, Stafford

Animals Poem

Birds fly overhead,
just as I said.
The cuckoo tells us it's spring,
while the wasp, it loves to sting.

Up on the hills are the sheep
who make a great flying leap.
Horses gallop over the hill,
hearing a lovely bird trill.

The song thrush sings up to the breeze;
squirrels run up into the leaves.
Aardvarks live in trees,
bees buzz around in the air
buzzing around by the bear.

In dive the dolphins, below the puffins,
the flying fish flies in the air, watching a lion in its lair.
The wobbegong shark, thinks it's a lark
while splashing around in the dark.
Down in the earth is a worm,
who likes to wriggle and squirm.

Abigail Carruthers (9)
Haberdashers' Redcap School, Hereford

Teachers And Child

The class is a horrible place
the children are such a disgrace
I'd rather not teach
but go to the beach
and get sunburn all over my face.

My teacher is called Mrs Pots
she's fat and she's covered in spots
she lets us play most of the day
but for homework she's giving us lots.

Sophie Wallis (10)
Haberdashers' Redcap School, Hereford

The Circus

Big, bright lights,
Focus on the yellow sand
The red curtain twitches
Noise grows louder,
As more people
Pile into seats.

Silence suddenly falls,
As the ringmaster
Walks grandly
Into the middle
Of the ring
'The show will now begin!'

Horses, acrobats,
Men and clowns.
People cheering,
Band screaming,
And then
The circus ends
And I walk out.

Elizabeth Keir (10)
Haberdashers' Redcap School, Hereford

Ocean Motion

Waves are banging on the rocks
Ocean spray floating on the wind

I am watching crashing waves
Watching fishing boats swapping crates

People sailing, people surfing
There are people everywhere

I see everyone laughing, having fun
How nice it must be to live by the sea.

Roisin Massam-Vallely (9)
Haberdashers' Redcap School, Hereford

Dolphins

I was looking around on the beach
When something caught my eye.
Something jumped out from the sea.
It was a shimmering blue animal
With a smooth body
And a pointed fin on its back.
Then I saw another and another.
Then I realised they were dolphins,
A group of them jumping and playing in the sea.
It was amazing, I loved seeing them all,
Then ever so quickly they swam away.

Kathryn Subak-Sharpe (10)
Haberdashers' Redcap School, Hereford

Sailing

Sailing on the calm sea,
Is just right,
Bobbing up and down,
Peacefully.

Steering the boat,
Further away,
Passing the beaches,
That the sea left behind.

But, sailing on the rough sea,
Is just terrible,
Going over the waves,
In a storm.

The rough waves,
Are sinking your boat,
Crash! goes the lightning,
As the rocks crumble.

Julia Watkinson (10)
Haberdashers' Redcap School, Hereford

Lunch Hall

In came the children,
Prancing about,
Laughing and talking then came a shout,
'Line up children, no talking, no chat!'
That's the head teacher over there, we call her Mrs Prat.
She's evil with horns
We'll tell you now, this is a warn,
She's been like this since she was born.
She can control the class,
She sets us very hard tasks,
She's a control freak and she likes to eat . . .
Children!

Florence Churchward (10)
Haberdashers' Redcap School, Hereford

Horses Are . . .

Horses are *fab!*
Horses are fast
Horses are fun
Horses are frisky
Horses are *fantastic!*

Emily Beckett (9)
Haberdashers' Redcap School, Hereford

What Am I?

Bone fetcher
Bottom sniffer
Cat chaser
Sloppy licker
Messy eater
Playful biter
What am I?

Sophie Nash (9)
Haberdashers' Redcap School, Hereford

Holidays

H is for holidays, playing in the sun, doing
    all sorts of things, you never know, it might snow.
O is for orange, the colour of the sand, blue and green are
    the colours of the sea, children laughing and making
    sandcastles, that's my idea of fun.
L is for lollies, yum-yum in my tum, for a very hot day,
    they melt in the sun and give the taste away.
I is for ice cream, yum-yum in my tum, different favours,
    different sauces, I don't know what I'll have.
D is for days filled with fun, you never know it might snow today,
    you go to the beach fun, fun for everyone.
A is for amazing, you will be amazed every day by the
    beautiful view and the sound of the beach.
Y is for yacht, they sail in the sea, they come to shore
    when they've had enough, they sail in the rain,
    they sail in the dark, they sail in any kind of weather.
S is for the sand, it's soft and slippery, sometimes it
    can be hot, but who cares? Flying a kite high in the sky,
    letting go and running after it. Oh no! I've let it go!

Francesca South (10)
Longden CE Primary School, Shrewsbury

The Seasons Of The Year

Spring is the time of year,
When all the flowers come out to play.
Summer is the time of year,
When all of the farmers crops are nearly fully grown.
Autumn is the time of year,
When all the leaves turn all sorts of colours and
Fall off the trees.
Winter is the time of year,
When it gets really cold and
All the children go *hooray!*

Adam Wagstaff (9)
Longden CE Primary School, Shrewsbury

The Trolls Beneath My Bunk Bed

There are trolls beneath my bunk bed,
Two of them at least,
One of them quite pleasant
And one's a brutal beast.

The one that seems quite nice,
She mends, fixes and cleans,
The other on the other hand,
He cries, bawls and screams.

While the girl is helpful,
As she washes, scrubs and sorts,
The boy's no use at all,
Picking at his warts.

But still the girl is busy
And the boy sits around all day,
They give me something special,
At night they come and play.

There are trolls beneath my bunk bed,
They're not a pretty sight,
But they give me something,
The time to play at night.

Emily-Jane Mitchell (9)
Longden CE Primary School, Shrewsbury

Ghost

The ghost floated through the house,
As quiet as a mouse,
She peered in at the sleeping child,
Thought for a while and smiled,
Memory and sadness filled her, the child began to stir,
Then with a swish like wind in clover,
The ghost disappeared, her time was over.

Abigail Nixon (10)
Longden CE Primary School, Shrewsbury

My Piebald Pony

Clippity clop, clippity clop, here comes my piebald pony,
He and I are a perfect pair, me and my piebald pony,
We ride like we own the world, me and my piebald pony,
He is a handsome gelding, my piebald pony.

His mane and tail blow in the wind, my piebald pony,
Fields we have trodden down, me and my piebald pony,
He is always there for me, my piebald pony,
He and I could take over the world, me and my piebald pony.

He eats all day, my piebald pony
And sleeps all night, my piebald pony,
His name is George, my piebald pony,
There goes, my piebald pony,
Off to eat again.

Rebecca Bruce (10)
Longden CE Primary School, Shrewsbury

My Mad Family

Baby screaming in her bed,
Mum and Gran have bumped their heads,
Brother falls,
Sister tripping over balls,
Cow goes moo,
Horse goes neigh,
All our chickens will not lay,
Mouse goes squeak,
Door goes creak,
When I'm testing, Dad takes a peek,
John is fighting poor little Emily,
Oh how will I live with this mad *family!*

Charlie Forth (10)
Longden CE Primary School, Shrewsbury

The Full Moon Baboon

When the full moon baboon comes out to play,
Be careful because the full moon baboon
Does a full moon baboon roar

And if you're not careful the full moon baboon might gobble,
Gibble, gobble you up!
So be careful when the full moon baboon comes out to play,
If a full moon baboon comes to your house …

Don't turn on the light,
It might give him a fright!

If you give a full moon baboon a fright …
Well it would not be a pleasant sight.

Meagan Roberts (11)
Longden CE Primary School, Shrewsbury

My Friend Jake

My friend Jake eats lots of cake,
He eats more cake,
Than his mum can bake,
One day he tried a hake-flavoured cake
Yuck!
He spat it right out,
After that he ate no more hake cake.

Sophie Rowson (9)
Longden CE Primary School, Shrewsbury

Jake

J is for Jake, that's my name,
A is for animals, I like to look after,
K is for Kathryn, that's who I sit by on my table,
E is for elephant, I would like to see.

Jake Roberts (10)
Longden CE Primary School, Shrewsbury

Tar Monster

T here's a tar monster on the playground.
A t hometime it eat kids, I've so far not been eaten,
R ob my friend got eaten yesterday, we're running out of kids.

M ore and more are being eaten, 20 children left and I'm one of them,
O n Wednesday I was eaten alive as I was walking home,
N ow I was trapped, the next day he swallowed someone's mum,
S cooby-Doo came to try and free me but ran away that day,
T o my luck, the tar monster was sick and me and Rob came out,
E ight days later, the tar monster exploded in the playground,
R ob and me celebrated the whole day through.

James Brayne (11)
Longden CE Primary School, Shrewsbury

Piranhas

If you fall in a river that's full of piranha,
They'll strip off your flesh like you'd skin a banana,
There's no time for cries, there's no time for groans,
For in forty-five seconds, you'll be nothing but bones!

Jessica Cox (9)
Longden CE Primary School, Shrewsbury

The Four-Eyed Girl

Yesterday I went to town,
I saw a girl in her dressing gown,
Not only did I see that,
There was something horrible underneath her hat,
I was just about to scream,
When I saw a horrible sight,
You'll never guess where I saw it,
It was embedded in her eye,
She was running straight towards me
And in the end, I screamed *aarrgghh!*

Ellie Jenkins (10)
Longden CE Primary School, Shrewsbury

Night-Time Fun

She sits on a chair of smoothest silk,
Eyes like jewels, gown like milk,
She gazes into the moonlit night
With stars aglow, it's really a sight,
She passed across an Angora rug,
Listens at the door and gives it a tug,
Her jewelled necklace glints like the sun,
She sets off through the house to have some fun,
She climbs the expensive velvet sofa
And claws the posh French bathroom loofah,
Knocks over bottles and bursts bags of flour,
When there's a noise upstairs, she does not cower,
The master comes down and turns on the light,
When he looks in the kitchen, the cat is a sight!

Holly Linford (11)
Longden CE Primary School, Shrewsbury

Winter

I really like winter
Because of all the fun
Snowball fights and the snow
Makes it really fun
When I go sledging
We go over humps
We go really fast and then we hurt our bums
We always have races
We go really fast
And when we get to the bottom
We build a snowman in the morning sun.

Lewis Jowett (10)
Longden CE Primary School, Shrewsbury

Cats And Dogs

Dog barks
Dog shakes
Dog eats
Mum's cakes.

Dog's mad
Dog bites
Dog catches
My kites.

Kittens play
Kittens sleep
Kittens like
To count sheep.

Kittens chase
Kittens catch
Kittens lie down
In a grass patch.

Daniel Rintoul (9)
Longden CE Primary School, Shrewsbury

My Annoying Brothers And Sister

My brother is a total bore
And when he sleeps he always snores,
My sister is a total nag
And when she is annoying it makes me mad.
My kitten Dwayne is a pain,
Especially when he shakes off rain,
My other brother is very mean
And somehow he likes baked beans,
As for me, I'm quite funny,
But I wouldn't be alive without my mummy!

Joel Pugh (9)
Longden CE Primary School, Shrewsbury

There's A Cow In The House

There's a cow in the house
And it's getting rather smelly,
It's big, black and white
And I can't see the telly.

I like to sing my opera
And when my song is sung,
I have to turn my attention
To shovelling out the dung.

But things aren't always bad
She sometimes fills us full of glee,
Especially when we squeeze her udders
To get milk for our cup of tea.

We wake early in the morning
As the cow begins to moo,
You can even hear her through the walls
As you've sat down on the loo.

Thomas Lear (9)
Longden CE Primary School, Shrewsbury

My Brother's Bouncy Ball

My brother got a new bouncy ball,
He thought that it would not bounce higher than two inches tall,
So he threw it his hardest at the floor,
It came back off the floor and went flying into the kitchen door,
It bounced off the pan and it hit the floor
And went back out of the door
And was not seen for evermore.

John Merrick (9)
Longden CE Primary School, Shrewsbury

Holidays

H olidays are brilliant, fun and fantastic,
O h when I was nine, I went to Disney Land,
L is for Lewis, he's been to Mexico and New Zealand,
I have been to Germany, I went there at the age of nine,
D ays on holiday are filled with fun and joy,
A ll your excitement fills your heart,
Y our days should be fun, your days should be great,
S ee if you can see the sea, go on a ferry,
                         I went on one to go to Holland.

Kathryn Adams (10)
Longden CE Primary School, Shrewsbury

On A Winter's Day

On a winter's day,
Playing in the garden,
Throwing snowballs at the wall,
Brother playing with his ball,
Nearly time to go for tea,
Then put up the Christmas tree,
Santa drinking cups of tea.

Lydia Ungless (7)
Milverton Primary School, Leamington Spa

There's Something In My Car

There's something in my car,
Oh it's a talking chocolate bar,
It's talking to me,
But how can it be,
I must be going bizarre!

Cameron Love (10)
Milverton Primary School, Leamington Spa

I Like My Bed

I like my bed because it's all cosy and warm,
I lie down in my bed with my cuddly toys
And I don't know what to dream about,
I ask my mum and dad to help me,
I have seven teeth out,
The tooth fairy whisks your teeth out,
The tooth fairy flies around like magic
With her sparkling wand,
My worse dreams are vampires and ghosts
And me and my family falling into a hole,
My best dream is me being with the BFG,
I like my duvet with colourful cats
And dark blue around and light blue for the squares,
I don't have my tooth under the pillow,
I have my tooth in a bowl on my bedside table.

Sophie Rowe (7)
Milverton Primary School, Leamington Spa

Winter And Spring

W inter is freezing cold,
 I t shivers in your arms,
N o one would ever know,
T hat under the snow,
E veryone is full of happiness,
R ising in the air.

S pring is when it gets warmer,
P loughing its way through the sky,
R oses blooming,
 I n the beautiful garden,
N ow wherever people go there is the
G littering golden sun, until it is winter again.

Natalie Gould (9)
Milverton Primary School, Leamington Spa

Moonshine Sunshine

The cold and the dull,
The warm and the bright,
The moon and the sun.

The sun shines and the moon shines,
Brightly one, the other dull,
One in the day, one in the night,
They turn each day to please the Earth.

The cold and the dull,
The warm and the bright,
The moon and the sun.

The Earth takes both for granted,
Although one day,
They might not be here
And neither will we.

The cold and the dull,
The warm and the bright,
The moon and the sun.

Neena Abdullah (11)
Milverton Primary School, Leamington Spa

Seasons!

Spring, summer, autumn, winter,
Every year's the same,
Round and round the seasons go,
Over and over again.

But sometimes I get bored
And it's a bit of a pain!
I'd like to change it so it
Didn't go over again!

Molly Minshull (10)
Milverton Primary School, Leamington Spa

My Original Season

I can feel the leaves crunching underfoot,
Whether gold or red, brown or orange, I don't know.
I can see the trees bending down, letting go of their heavy leaves,
Whether oak or birch, horse chestnut or beech, I don't know,
I can hear a bird crying out from its nest,
Whether black or robin, crow or kestrel, I don't know,
This is my idea of autumn, cool but peaceful, sharp
But happy this is my original autumn.

I can feel the snow cracking underfoot,
Whether old or new, thin or thick, I don't know,
I can see the cottage with a pure white roof,
Whether warm or cold, abandoned or living, I don't know,
I can hear the happy cry of children in the glittering park,
Whether scared and joyful, miserable or excited, I don't know,
This is my idea of winter, freezing but warm,
Joyful and peaceful: this is my original winter!

Anne Devereux (9)
Milverton Primary School, Leamington Spa

The Lion And The Pussycat

(Inspired by 'The Owl and the Pussycat' by Edward Lear)

The lion and the pussycat went to sea,
In a beautiful purple boat,
They took some money and plenty of dummies
Wrapped in a beautiful coat.
The lion looked up at the stars above
And sang on a small cigar,
'Oh smelly pussy, oh pussy my dove,
What an ugly pussy you are,
You are,
You are!
What an ugly pussy you are!'

Aidan Bradbury (10)
Milverton Primary School, Leamington Spa

White Horses

White horses, white horses,
White horses, everywhere.

You can find them in the moors,
Galloping through the wind.

You can also find them at the beach
Galloping over the waves.

You can also find them on the clouds,
Galloping over the puff under the starry sky.

But out of all of them,
My favourite is called Misty.

Heidi Roberts (9)
Milverton Primary School, Leamington Spa

Summer

S un gleaming in our eyes,
U mbrellas shading on the sand,
M ums relaxing giving us money for ice cream,
M ules giving children rides for just £1,
E veryone having fun,
R unning into the sea.

Lauren Pugh (10)
Milverton Primary School, Leamington Spa

Future

F ast, underwater flying cars,
U p in space with the stars,
T wo skis that work on water,
U p in the air in your chair,
R ight down under the ground,
E verything's *brilliant!*

Gabrielle Calvert (9)
Milverton Primary School, Leamington Spa

Me, My Mate And Shane

Me and my mate,
Went to Spain,
The plane was late,
In the lounge we met Shane,
We ran to the gate,
Finally we got on the plane,
In the morning we arrived at 8.

We bought some sweets,
We ate them real quick,
We bought a CD of Keets,
We were all sick!
You could say we threw up
And that was the beginning of our holiday luck!

Hannah Pope (10)
Milverton Primary School, Leamington Spa

Uncle Moe

There is someone at the door,
I wonder who it can be?
He's not going to go,
So I'd better go and see,
It is uncle Moe,
He's come to see me
And guess what he's brought,
A chimpanzee!
Then he came in for coffee and tea,
But then he left
And I wish he would come back.

Oliver Murray (10)
Milverton Primary School, Leamington Spa

The Wavy Sea

The wavy sea, the wavy sea,
Is so cold just like an icicle.

The wavy sea, the wavy sea,
Is so dark and blue,
Just like the chairs in our classroom.

The wavy sea, the wavy sea,
It is really beautiful,
Like a diamond in a shop window.

Oh how lovely the sea,
Oh how nice and wet,
The sea is wonderfully warm.

Rory Barber (9)
Milverton Primary School, Leamington Spa

Mingled Smells

Mingled smells, mingled smells,
One is Daddy's socks!
Another is Mum's washing powder
And a muddy fox, *hay!*

Mingled smells, mingled smells,
We have to go to the market,
But then came up, a rather old cop
And told us to properly park it,
The car!

David Fairbairn (9)
Milverton Primary School, Leamington Spa

Me And My Friend

Me and my friend went to Spain,
It was tipping down with rain.

I didn't like it, I won't ever go again,
I really want to go to my house,
Because I'm missing my pet mouse.

My mouse's name is Hen,
But my brother's name is Ben.

I don't like my brother Ben,
Because he always laughs at my mouse Hen.

Yousef Hanif (11)
Milverton Primary School, Leamington Spa

The Sea Spies

The sea spies, with their five lumpy legs,
With their star-shaped bodies.
They only lie down, for they cannot stand,
They slowly move through the water,
Gliding on the sparkling sand,
They are very camouflaged and . . .
They spy on the people above them!
Though they're really quite nice,
Even though they spy!
They only lie down,
They cannot stand, or fly!

Abigail Watt (9)
Milverton Primary School, Leamington Spa

There Was Once A Man Called Moat

There was once a man called Moat,
He sailed to sea in a boat,
He took with him a bottle of gin
And a very warm coat.

On his travels, Moat met some camels,
That made him laugh out loud,
But that was when disaster came,
With the big black cloud.

He stayed inside and lost his mind
Drank too much gin
And . . . that was the end of him.

Harry Conway (10)
Milverton Primary School, Leamington Spa

Holiday In Spain

Me and Reed Paine
Went to Spain
On our private jet plane
We took lots of sweets and ate them too quick
And a few minutes later, we were suddenly sick.

When we finally got there
We went to a butcher and bought a hare,
But the strange thing was it wasn't dead,
So after that we went to bed.

George Lambert (10)
Milverton Primary School, Leamington Spa

I Can't Wait

I can't wait for Portugal,
I can't wait for the sun,
I can't wait for the sand,
I can't wait for the sea.

I can't wait for anything!

My family can't wait for Portugal,
My family can't wait for the sun,
My family can't wait for the sand,
My family can't wait for the sea.

My family can't wait for anything!

Maisie Tudge (9)
Milverton Primary School, Leamington Spa

My Cat Gypsy

There's something in the caravan,
I wonder what it could be,
Oh, it's my cat Gypsy,
How silly of me,
Nothing's in her tummy
And as usual seems hungry,
She's as black as can be,
Now she's coming home with me!

Alexander Bennell (9)
Milverton Primary School, Leamington Spa

War Of Man

Before all of it, we dug a deep trench,
Oh what a terrible stench!
When we had finished,
Planes being built to fly,
For a soldier will cry,
With pain, pain of death,
'My fellow friend,' I called,
Will I live through all of this? I thought.
'Do you think?' With bread,
A stew and fruit, we say,
Have enough energy to fight?
Later on I heard the sound of an
English plane, flying to France,
Days later, I took my chance,
My fellow soldiers stood ready for the French,
But it was like war on a bench,
For they did not come . . . until . . .
Suddenly they came on planes,
Flying as quickly as they could,
I was ready in my plane,
Flying with my fellow soldiers . . . and then
I was forced to fly solo by the French,
Seconds later, I was hit and . . .
And help!

Luis Alarcon (9)
Milverton Primary School, Leamington Spa

My Mum Is Number One

With a caring heart and long curly hair,
When I'm in trouble, I know she'll be there,
Her eyes are brown with a glint so bright
And she teaches me what is wrong or right.
She gives me books and toys and food
And she loves me even if I'm in a bad mood.
If I fall over, she'll help me mop my knees,
She taught me my first words, 'Thank you' and 'Please'.
She can be bossy, that I must admit,
But I don't care at all, not one bit!
She bathed me and fed me and gave me clothes to wear,
She taught me little lessons and taught me how to share,
She reads me bedtime stories and tucks me in at night
But never disagree with her cause Mum is always right.

OK she isn't perfect but to me she is the best,
If there was a competition, then she would win the test!

Joanna Lam (10)
Our Lady & St Werburgh's RC School, Newcastle

Teachers

Teachers are the best,
Even though I'm a pest,
I'm *sooo* cool,
I rule my school.

I terrify the dinner ladies,
Their food is always gross,
It tastes like washing up liquid,
To be honest, I'd rather eat a piece of toast.

Katie Bullock (10)
Our Lady & St Werburgh's RC School, Newcastle

Story Time

Be quiet little children
Don't say a word
It's story time now
You should be seen and not heard,
Sit on the floor, not on the chair,
Milly, please stop cutting your hair.
Do you want to hear what happened to me yesterday?
Oh stop moaning or go away,
Alfred sit down, I was only joking,
Betty put that back, stop pretending to be smoking,
What story shall I tell today?
Oh come on children, please say,
It's not normally this quiet,
You're always a big riot.

Sophie Bunting (10)
Our Lady & St Werburgh's RC School, Newcastle

My Puppy Monty

My puppy Monty is so cute,
He chews everything up,
We haven't got a digital remote now
Since the day he ate it up.

Monty is a rascal,
He is so cheeky,
But I love him still,
Even though he's a little monkey.

Monty loves tennis balls,
But they roll away,
Under the gate and out of reach
And I have to go and fetch them.

(If he climbs on the furniture again, Mum will skin him!)

Rachel Sherwin (10)
Our Lady & St Werburgh's RC School, Newcastle

Birtie Blob

Mr Blob is such a slob,
His nails are always dirty,
He's such a scruff, his beard is rough
And he's only going on thirty.

He shuffles around with his feet on the ground,
In shoes that are always dirty,
His shirt hangs out as he slouches about
And his first name is Birtie.

His feet smell of cheese, his socks have fleas,
You can't be around him with any ease,
He's in Class 8 which is always a state,
Don't put me in that class please!

Ruairidh McKenna (10)
Our Lady & St Werburgh's RC School, Newcastle

My Little Sister

My little sister Millie, she is so very sweet,
She wears pretty dresses and looks very neat,
Her hair's a lovely flowing blonde,
She thinks the boys are pretty fond,
Her eyes are a blue so bright,
She proves me wrong when we have a little fight,
She loves to go to school and also loves to play,
She's got so much energy and could run about all day,
She is so bubbly,
The bubbliest person I know,
She's a little drama queen and is great in a show,
She throws a tantrum and makes a lot of noise,
Then stomps up to her bedroom and throws about her toys,
I love my little sister,
Although she can be,
A bit of a tinker and I'm sure that she loves me.

Harriet Allbutt (10)
Our Lady & St Werburgh's RC School, Newcastle

My Brother Jake

My brother Jake is such a pain!
I suppose that's just his surname,
He's as red as a tomato with all his spots,
But he's always such a clumsy clots!
He slumps around all day
And he's got so much money to pay!
Jake's my brother
He's such a div,
That's just how
I have to live!

Holly Payne (10)
Our Lady & St Werburgh's RC School, Newcastle

My Cousin Bethan

My cousin Bethan has a kind heart,
If I had to describe her I wouldn't know where to start.
She has silky brown hair and lots of nice things to wear,
When I am alone, she is always there,
I always think of her twanging her hair,
She has a little sister Eva,
Whose nickname is Eva the beaver,
My cousin Bethan goes to ballet,
When we go round we play,
She has a cat called Jake
And the cat likes milkshake.

B ubbly and bouncy that is what she is like,
E ager and exciting, and likes to ride her bike,
T errific and talkative, that's what she does,
H appy and hilarious, that's what she loves,
A dventurous and active, that's how she lives,
N aughty and nice, that's what she is like.

Megan Nolan (10)
Our Lady & St Werburgh's RC School, Newcastle

My Brother Danny

My brother Danny
Is so fun, sometimes we argue,
Sometimes we don't.

So this is my brother,
Going on camp,
Goes in the wood,
Can't stop him from getting muddy.

At home with my mum
Boring stuff,
Guess what it was
Food shopping.

Don't want to go
Dan doesn't have to,
So why do I?

Coming back,
Sat in the car,
Nothing to do.

Charlotte Counter (10)
Our Lady & St Werburgh's RC School, Newcastle

The Wedding

Holly and Jake got married
On the playground one day
Scott did the honours
We told him what to say,
She had a ring of daisies,
It was all so very sweet,
In her uniform so neat,
We formed a first class aeroplane,
For them to honeymoon in Spain,
We certainly had a lot of fun,
On that sunny day in year one.

Jessica Scally (10)
Our Lady & St Werburgh's RC School, Newcastle

My Sister Tilly Rose

Tilly's so sweet but can defeat,
She likes her bear but pulls my hair,
She loves pearls but hates other girls,
She's always up and about but never down and out,
Up and round she plays clowns,
Lipstick happy, smiley stuff,
Those are the things that keep her chuffed.
Mum, Dad, Oliver and Jade,
She loves them but sometimes makes them her maids.
She is the queen of our house,
So we thought we would crown her mouse,
But now she is growing up and
It brings a tear to my eye,
To see my little sister cry.

Jade Ely (10)
Our Lady & St Werburgh's RC School, Newcastle

My Little Brother

My little brother has short blond hair,
If I'm lonely I know he'll be there,
His eyes are blue and sparkle in the light,
He's always happy and very, very bright,
He's sometimes strong and proves me wrong
But our arguments are never long,
He likes chocolate, biscuits and sweets,
He loves people giving him treats,
He loves to paint, he loves to play,
He could run and jump in the mud all day,
When I see him sleeping at night,
I want to hug and cuddle him tight.

Marisha Monaghan (11)
Our Lady & St Werburgh's RC School, Newcastle

Ella

(For Ella, I love you)

When will she be here?
I can't wait to see,
Mum says I can hold her and bounce her on my knee.
She's going to be so sweet,
Her dress will be so neat,
We will play all day long,
Then we will sing her a lovely song
And I have made lots of things
And a bracelet made out of strings.
I will take her for walks in her lovely pram,
Then I will give her a toy, a lovely little lamb,
Then she will have a nap
And I'll cuddle her on my lap,
We will go to the park and then it will get dark,
When the sun goes down and the moon comes up for the night,
I'll tuck her up in bed and whisper in her ear,
I love you, sleep tight.

Megan McCoy (10)
Our Lady & St Werburgh's RC School, Newcastle

The Rain

I go pitter-patter on your window
Wetting you through,
Umbrellas won't stop me
You never know when I will fall
If you want to stay dry
Stay inside.

When I stop, the sun comes out,
Children come out to play,
Everyone is happy for the
Rest of the day.

Tayyibah Patel (10)
Queens CE Junior School, Nuneaton

The Tree

I can bring birds and animals towards me,
I can make a flower grow around me,
Bringing a sweet smell towards me,
I can light the world around me,
By just breathing out fresh air.

I can bring sweetness to our valley,
Making a rainbow shine above us,
I can treat you well if you need any help,
I can give you shade and shelter,
But don't come to me when there's lightning,
As I can be very *dangerous* with my arms of electricity.

I can make you feel much better,
When you come to me,
I can massage your back so smoothly,
Just come to me and you'll see,
I am the tree.

Amani Ismail (11)
Queens CE Junior School, Nuneaton

The Sun

I am a nurse, healing people with my warmth,
I am a footballer, teasing you by never showing my face,
I am a child, hugging you with my warmth,
I can be dark and rusty or I can bring happiness,
I can reach the ground and speak to people,
I am sitting on the ground in my nightgown
I am sitting on the ground in my nightgown
I have got long hair to my feet,
I drew a picture for my friend,
I am the sun.

Alison House
Queens CE Junior School, Nuneaton

Fire

I can torture the forest,
With my arms of destruction,
I can knock down a house,
With my bright orange blaze,
Have you guessed who I am yet?
Are you sure?

I am fire!

Alison Hughes
Queens CE Junior School, Nuneaton

The Sun

I shine like a star,
I shine all day long,
I shine on the Earth,
Making everyone happy all day long,
I can see happy people
And everyone is happy,
I can burn and scorch.

Gemma Campbell
Queens CE Junior School, Nuneaton

The Tree

I can suffocate the juveniles,
With my winding legs,
I can home the homeless,
With my caring arms,
I can brighten the countryside,
With my lush green clothes,
I am a tree.

Marcus Holt (10)
Queens CE Junior School, Nuneaton

The Sun

I can make the flowers grow
With my arms I can grab the moon,
And tell him to stay away,
I can get you with my yellow eye.

I can make you feel thirsty,
In the hot, hot weather,
I can make you hungry,
When I make a rainbow.

I can weave in-between you,
With my long hot legs,
If I ever touch you,
I will hurt you with my orange flaming hands of fire.

I am an octopus,
Reaching up with my long tentacles,
I suck up all the sand on the land
And all the fish in the sea.

I am the sun!

Jessica Tandy (10)
Queens CE Junior School, Nuneaton

The Rain

If I am light people love me
Flowers drink me
Splashing in my puddles
When I am heavy I flood the street
People go inside
They don't want to play with me anymore.
One good thing,
Mum and Dad won't have to water the plants today.

Amy Marshall (10)
Queens CE Junior School, Nuneaton

The Wind

I blow all day long
From sunlight to darkness
I blow your washing dry
I can cause many deaths

I smash all your cities
I can give you a breeze
I make people shiver
And I cause destruction

The roots are torn out by me
I am twisters and hurricanes
I don't really mean to hurt
But sometimes I just lash out.

Jamie Slack (10)
Queens CE Junior School, Nuneaton

The Sun

I can bring you warmth
And deliver you light
I can cause dehydration
All day and night.

I am the biggest star
I am a giant fireball
I'm the nearest star to the Earth
I deliver light to the world.

I can make you happy,
Giving you warmth
I can make you happy
Giving you light.

Connor Fletcher
Queens CE Junior School, Nuneaton

The Rain

I can make your plants grow,
I can make your crops emerge,
Some of my showers are good,
But some aren't.

I can cause floods,
I can produce hurricanes with wind,
So stay inside,
Unless you want to die.

When I'm angry,
I will strike.

Umar Aswat (10)
Queens CE Junior School, Nuneaton

The Rain

I can gently shower,
Or fiercely dive,
I can wet you,
Drown you.

I can gently shower,
Or cruelly dive,
By staying away,
I can cause a drought.

I can gently shower,
Or wildly dive,
I can water your plants,
Or drown your flowers.

Jack Jones
Queens CE Junior School, Nuneaton

The Rain

I am the rain
I am bad.
I go pitter-patter
On your window

I hail on people,
People run inside
And never come out

If you want to
Stay dry,
Stay inside.

Adil Shaikh
Queens CE Junior School, Nuneaton

The Snow

The snow cuddles the mossy tree,
As it sprints across the white snowy field,
The snow lands on its feet as it falls off the mossy tree.

The snow jogs along the field
And plays hide-and-seek with the grass,
The snow gets drowsy and falls asleep,
The snow swims as it melts.

Leah Stringer
Queens CE Junior School, Nuneaton

The Sun

I feel very hot
I see people with umbrellas looking for shade.

I can melt ice cream with one of my flames.
I see people in outer space.

Rizwaan Dawood
Queens CE Junior School, Nuneaton

The Rain

I fall on you
When you're not expecting me
If you're not wearing a coat
Prepare to get wet.

I bring wetness to the world
I stop droughts from happening

I can do a cracking storm
I feel respected by some animals
Especially fish, frogs and ducks
I feel happy
When everyone's happy and safe.

Gemma Mann
Queens CE Junior School, Nuneaton

The Dark Alley

I am dark and scary
I see a lot who've died
I use arms to help the wounded
I help children through me,
So people will not hurt them
I use my arms of soap to clean me in the dark.

Jack Gwilliam (10)
Queens CE Junior School, Nuneaton

The Darkness

I sit in empty corners and lie underneath your beds,
I stand in a lot of cupboards to put on my clothes,
I walk up alleys and up the walls in the bins,
I slide down the drainpipes and in the sewage,
I am darkness.

Lewis Wilkinson (11)
Queens CE Junior School, Nuneaton

The Sun

I can sweep away the darkness,
With my arms of love,
I can mend the broken hearted,
By sharing warmth with you,
I can take good care of you,
With my eyes that see everything,
I can burn away the sadness without any tears,
I am the sun!

Saddaf Caratella (10)
Queens CE Junior School, Nuneaton

The Sun

I bring warmth all day long
I see children playing
I see ice melting
I hear horns beeping
I hear birds singing
I blaze into your room
I stare right at your wall
I help to make flowers.

Stephanie Mason (11)
Queens CE Junior School, Nuneaton

The Sea

I can be calm and nice,
Watch me roll my waves one by one.
I make waves for surfers,
Watch me as I do my things.
Because of the happiness,
Watch me as I go up and down.

I am the sea.

Gemma Nicholson (10)
Queens CE Junior School, Nuneaton

The Sun

I am a nurse, healing people with my warmth,
I am a footballer, teasing you by never showing my face,
I am a child, hugging you with my warmth,
I can be dark and rusty or I can bring happiness,
I can reach the ground in my nightgown,
I have got long hair to my feet,
I drew a picture for my friend,
I am the sun.

Faizah Khalifa
Queens CE Junior School, Nuneaton

A Tree/A Teenager

I am a teenager,
I'm too tired to move,
My arms are like sticks of rock,
My legs are stuck to the ground,
And I'm fed up,
I don't want to be moved,
I am a tree.

Chelsey McKenzie (10)
Queens CE Junior School, Nuneaton

The Moon

I can look after you and
Follow you around.
I can put the light on,
When it is dark.
I am the moon.

Jalaluddin Musa
Queens CE Junior School, Nuneaton

The Galaxy

The darkness of its roots makes the swirling black holes,
The sun burns away meteorites like fire burning coal,
The planets float around in our galaxy,
A black hole eats the planets like a creature eating me,
The Earth runs around the sun in one year,
Mars is a darker planet which has a darker year,
Pluto is a really ice-cold planet,
The sun dies down in the middle of the year.

Glenn Tweed (10)
Queens CE Junior School, Nuneaton

The Sun

I can sweep the darkness away,
I can wrap my warmth around people,
I can make you feel happy with my gleaming smile,
I can bandage you up with my heat,
I can burn away the sadness without any tears.

I am the sun.

Nasreen Fatuwala (11)
Queens CE Junior School, Nuneaton

The Dog

I am a little boy, playing with my ball,
I am playing with my friends running around freely,

I am like the wind running very fast
As fast as sound I would say,
I am like an old man sleeping most of the day
In my nice coat.

James Walden
Queens CE Junior School, Nuneaton

The Snow

Like white crystals from sky,
Covering the ground with a thick white blanket,
Dancing above the trees.

Looking at people through the window,
It falls asleep on the ground,
Cuddling the hard rough trees,
Hopping around the wind.

Jamie Collins (10)
Queens CE Junior School, Nuneaton

The Galaxy

The galaxy is a dark place,
With planets flying in circles.
The sun attacks the comets
While the black hole sucks up its catch.
When the moon floats up,
The sun falls down.

Aadam Shaikh
Queens CE Junior School, Nuneaton

The Rain

The rain hammers down on the rooftops,
It springs across fields with the wind,
It writes a message on the pavement,
The cloud throws rain on the passing umbrellas,
The rain looks down at the beautiful ground,
The rain creeps up on unsuspecting people.

Tom Sewell (11)
Queens CE Junior School, Nuneaton

The Snow

Snow will eat the trees' leaves,
Snow will talk to the cars,
The snow will whistle with the trees,
Snow will leap when it's falling,
Snow shimmers in the starlight,
Snowflakes sing on the treetops,

Snow will cry when people walk on it,
Snow walks quietly across the playground,
Snow snores while sleeping on the ground,
Snow will wave to the robins above,
Snow will hunt for ground to lie on,
Snow will cuddle the bottom of a tree.

Gemma Harris (10)
Queens CE Junior School, Nuneaton

Lightning

She writes a message to her friends,
She jumps out all of a sudden,
And strikes her shiny sword at the clouds,
Speeding through the sky.

She laughs so much she has to rest,
After playing chase with her mates,
She flashes her light through the sky,
Blinding the mice that run by.

Stephanie Hurleston (11)
Queens CE Junior School, Nuneaton

Star

The star comes at night,
Showing her blinding light,
She scares all the mice at night,
She writes a message to her friends.

She cries when it's morning,
She shouts to the moon when it's time go to back down,
She prays the day goes fast,
In the day she sleeps so silently,
At nightfall she is in luck,
She has a quick party and goes back up.

Lauren Garnham (10)
Queens CE Junior School, Nuneaton

Stars

They write a secret message,
Some hide behind a cloud,
They cover each other warmly,
They're never very loud.

They sleep very silently,
Cuddling up to the moon,
The clouds make a warm bed for them,
They fall asleep very soon.

Inayah Ghumra (10)
Queens CE Junior School, Nuneaton

The Wind

The wind slams the gate shut,
Like an angry crocodile,
Whistling wind like a bird whistling,
Howling wind just like a wolf alone,
Whining wind like a lonely dog.

Rebecca Barr (10)
Queens CE Junior School, Nuneaton

In The Playground

Teachers sobbed,
'Be quiet.'

Boys groaned,
'I've hurt myself.'

Trees moaned,
'They're better than us.'

Girls screamed,
'Help, they are getting us.'

Adam Cox (7)
Rokeby Junior School, Rugby

In The Playground

Gutters shatter,
'Stop blowing.'
Boys boasted,
'I run better.'
Boys groaned,
'Stop throwing.'

Vivek Solanki (7)
Rokeby Junior School, Rugby

In The Playground

Trees whispered
Benches squeaked
Bags moaned
Bins boasted
Hedges rustled
People kicked people.

Joshua Foster (7)
Rokeby Junior School, Rugby

In The Playground

Doors shouted,
'Leave me alone now!'

Boys roared,
'Come here.'

Grass bellowed,
'Get off me!'

Trees whispered,
'Hello children.'

Scott Collins (7)
Rokeby Junior School, Rugby

In The Playground

Doors cried,
'Stop banging me.'
Boys shouted,
'Let's play.'
Bins groaned,
'I am sore.'
Balls screamed,
'Stop kicking me.'

Oliver Griffiths-Jones (7)
Rokeby Junior School, Rugby

In The Playground

Trees whispered
Benches squeaked
Bags moaned
Bins boasted.

Aston Gibbons (7)
Rokeby Junior School, Rugby

In The Playground

Benches squeaked,
'Get off me.'

Trees whispered
'I like my leaves.'

Bags moaned
'Stop kicking me.'

Bins boasted,
'Stop sitting on me.'

Georgia Tailby (8)
Rokeby Junior School, Rugby

In The Playground

Trees whispered,
'I'm old.'

Coats sobbed,
'Our arms ache.'

Squirrels cheered,
'Hooray!'

Doors yelled,
'That hurt!'

Kira Fraser (7)
Rokeby Junior School, Rugby

In The Playground

Paths sobbed,
'Stop walking all over me.'

Mums shouted,
'Oh, stop it!'

Girls screamed,
'Argh, argh, argh!'

Boys cried,
'Stop it.'

Doors muttered,
'Oi!'

Brittany Roberts (8)
Rokeby Junior School, Rugby

In The Playground

Doors shouted
'Stop slamming me.'
Teachers moaned,
'Be quiet.'
Bags cried,
'Stop throwing me.'
Balls complained,
'Stop me from rolling.'

Courtney Smith (7)
Rokeby Junior School, Rugby

In The Playground

Grass whispered,
'This is the life.'

Bench cried,
'Stop sitting on me.'

Girls suggested,
'Let's annoy the boys.'

Squirrels boasted,
'Look at the hideous children!'

Poppy Douglas (7)
Rokeby Junior School, Rugby

In The Playground

Benches squeaked,
'Stop sitting on my head.'

Trees whispered,
'I like being in the breeze.'

Bags moaned,
'Stop throwing me at that tree.'

Bins boasted,
'Hey, we are better than you!'

Lara Furness (7)
Rokeby Junior School, Rugby

In The Playground

Doors yelled
Girls boasted
Benches moaned
Squirrels groaned
Boys shouted
Slides sobbed.

Caitlin Slade (7)
Rokeby Junior School, Rugby

In The Playground

Boys screamed,
'Give me the football.'

Trees muttered,
'It's windy today.'

Path howled,
'Sweep me up please.'

Doors groaned,
'Stop banging me.'

Bethany Pockley (7)
Rokeby Junior School, Rugby

In The Playground

Trees whispered,
'It's quiet round here.'

The playground complained,
'They are always standing on us!'

Grass moaned,
'I don't like it when they run over us.'

Boys boasted,
'We're better than you.'

Hollie Watts (7)
Rokeby Junior School, Rugby

In The Playground

Teachers sighed,
'Stop playing with pencils.'

Robins yelled,
'They are rocking our trees.'

Girls shrieked,
'Let's play.'

Children screamed,
'This is fun.'

Jenna Smith (8)
Rokeby Junior School, Rugby

In The Playground

Doors moaned,
'Stop slamming me.'

Teachers sobbed,
'Don't do that.'

Bags groaned,
'Stop it!'

Gutter boasted,
'We are better.'

Paige Richardson (8)
Rokeby Junior School, Rugby

In The Playground

Teachers roared,
'Listen carefully.'

Doors growled,
'You are so annoying.'

Bags yelled,
'Owwwww!'

Squirrels shrieked,
'I like children.'

Charlotte Kelly (7)
Rokeby Junior School, Rugby

In The Playground

Doors muttered,
'Stop opening and shutting me.'

Teachers moaned,
'Stop hitting people.'

Bags groaned,
'Don't throw me.'

Squirrels boasted,
'We're way better than them.'

Kieran Mistry (7)
Rokeby Junior School, Rugby

It Was So Quiet

It was so quiet that I heard
a little spider munch on a juicy fly.
It was so quiet that I heard
a tiny spider spin a lovely web.
It was so quiet that I heard
a great butterfly flutter in the sky.
It was so quiet that I heard
slimy snail slither along the ground.
It was so quiet that I heard
a feathery bird glide through the air.
It was so quiet that I heard
a wet tear run down my face.
It was so quiet that I heard
a fluffy cloud blow across the sky.
It was so quiet that I heard
a shiny star twinkle in the big blue sky.

Sophie Hillier (8)
SS Peter & Paul's Catholic Primary School, Lichfield

It Was So Quiet

It was so quiet that I heard a little snail
crawling along the garden path.
It was so quiet that I heard a brown seed
growing in the ground.
It was so quiet that I heard a sad tear
dropping down my cheek.
It was so quiet that I heard a clever idea
jump into my head.
It was so quiet that I heard a soft cloud
floating in the sky.

Kyle Gadsby, Olivia Willmore (8),
Jamie Checkland & Callum Bryant (7)
SS Peter & Paul's Catholic Primary School, Lichfield

It Was So Quiet

It was so quiet that I heard
a tiny black spider talk to me.
It was so quiet that I heard
a mini spider crawl across the path.
It was so quiet that I heard
a spotty spider spin its gorgeous web.
It was so quiet that I heard
a cute little spider chew some yummy food.
It was so quiet that I heard
a silky spider scream for food.
It was so quiet that I heard
a twinkling star shine in the sky.
It was so quiet that I heard
a tiny blue raindrop fall from the sky.
It was so quiet that I heard
a soft white snowflake twisting from the sky.

Imogen Finkle (8)
SS Peter & Paul's Catholic Primary School, Lichfield

It Was So Quiet

It was so quiet that I heard
my cute guinea pig rustle around to find some food.
It was so quiet that I heard
a rainbow sprout out of the ground.
It was so quiet that I heard
a cold snowflake sparkling in the dark sky.
It was so quiet that I heard
a spotty spider crawl across my room.
It was so quiet that I heard
a sparkling spinning star shoot across the sky.
It was so quiet that I heard
a brown seed sprout up out of the earth into a sunflower.
It was so quiet that I heard
a black ant crawl across my garden on the path.
It was so quiet that I heard
a shining raindrop fall from the light sky.

Charlotte Richards (7)
SS Peter & Paul's Catholic Primary School, Lichfield

It Was So Quiet

It was so quiet that I heard
a small spider crawling across the floor.
It was so quiet that I heard
a brown seed falling in the ground.
It was so quiet that I heard
a tiny star firing through the air.
It was so quiet that I heard
a white cloud throwing rain.
It was so quiet that I heard
a slow snail slithering across the ground.
It was so quiet that I heard
a cold snowflake falling down.
It was so quiet that I heard
a little ant scuttling across the path.
It was so quiet that I heard
a spotty ladybird flying over my head.

Kkyan Dunét (8)
SS Peter & Paul's Catholic Primary School, Lichfield

It Was So Quiet

It was so quiet that I heard
a little butterfly flutter across the sky.
It was so quiet that I heard
a small feather fall on the ground.
It was so quiet that I heard
a tiny page flicker.
It was so quiet that I heard
a huge tree drink clear water.
It was so quiet that I heard
water freeze into an ice cube.
It was so quiet that I heard
a small ant's tummy rumble.
It was so quiet that I heard
a baby ghost run away.
It was so quiet that I heard
the soft wind sweep across my face.

Tonicha Southern (8)
SS Peter & Paul's Catholic Primary School, Lichfield

It Was So Quiet

It was so quiet that I heard
a little fly talking.
It was so quiet that I heard
a pin dropping on a carpet.
It was so quiet that I heard
a beautiful snowflake forming in the clouds.
It was so quiet that I heard
the huge Earth turning in space.
It was so quiet that I heard
a small fly bumping into a web.
It was so quiet that I heard
a fluffy cloud floating in the sky.
It was so quiet that I heard
a tiny ladybird fluttering off my hand.
It was so quiet that I heard
a rainbow bending in the sky.

Ben Cross (8)
SS Peter & Paul's Catholic Primary School, Lichfield

It Was So Quiet

It was so quiet that I heard
a little racing star.
It was so quiet that I heard
a yellow spider look at the sun.
It was so quiet that I heard
a fluffy cloud running through the sky.
It was so quiet that I heard
a snowflake looking at the quiet sky.
It was so quiet that I heard
a ladybird with a tear coming down her face.
It was so quiet that I heard
a shining star shining in the sky.
It was so quiet that I heard
a rainbow dancing in the sky.
It was so quiet that I heard
a snail running in the sun.

Jordana Thatcher (8)
SS Peter & Paul's Catholic Primary School, Lichfield

It Was So Quiet

It was so quiet that I heard
a beautiful butterfly fluttering in the sky.
It was so quiet that I heard
a little ant creep down the path.
It was so quiet that I heard
a tiny spider spin its beautiful web.
It was so quiet that I heard
a white snowflake floating to the ground.
It was so quiet that I heard
a tiny tear softly fall down my cheek.
It was so quiet that I heard
a spotty ladybird just about to flutter in the sky.
It was so quiet that I heard
the colours of the rainbow appear in the sky.
It was so quiet that I heard
this poem slip into my head.

Poppy McMulkin (8)
SS Peter & Paul's Catholic Primary School, Lichfield

It Was So Quiet

It was so quiet that I heard
a green leaf floating on the cold wind.
It was so quiet that I heard
a tiny ant scurry across the ground.
It was so quiet that I heard
a cold teardrop running down my face.
It was so quiet that I heard
a beautiful flower growing through the earth.
It was so quiet that I heard
the warm breeze spinning around.
It was so quiet that I heard
a colourful rainbow rising up in the sky.
It was so quiet that I heard
my clever brain thinking of all good ideas.
It was so quiet that I heard
my nails growing on my finger.

Rebecca Hutchings (7)
SS Peter & Paul's Catholic Primary School, Lichfield

It Was So Quiet

It was so quiet that I heard
a cold ice cube melt in my drink.
It was so quiet that I heard
a fly fluttering its wings.
It was so quiet that I heard
a big pencil scratching across my page.
It was so quiet that I heard
a fat snail sliding across the wet grass.
It was so quiet that I heard
blue water wobbling in a glass.
It was so quiet that I heard
a little bug running across the ground.
It was so quiet that I heard
a brown seed whooshing out of the grass.
It was so quiet that I heard
a black bug nibbling my big black shoe.

Rebecca Prentice (8)
SS Peter & Paul's Catholic Primary School, Lichfield

It Was So Quiet

It was so quiet that I heard
a black spider spinning in a web.
It was so quiet that I heard
a red ladybird looking for some food.
It was so quiet that I heard
a shooting star appear.
It was so quiet that I heard
a fly bumping into my window.
It was so quiet that I heard
a floating cloud fly.
It was so quiet that I heard
the sun shining on the ground.
It was so quiet that I heard
a spotty snail slithering on the window.
It was so quiet that I heard
a tear dropping on my cheek.

Matthew Dale (7)
SS Peter & Paul's Catholic Primary School, Lichfield

It Was So Quiet

It was so quiet that I heard
a black ant crawling across a leaf.
It was so quiet that I heard
a red ladybird flying across by my window.
It was so quiet that I heard
a colourful rainbow shining in the sky.
It was so quiet that I heard
a flashing star high in the sky.
It was so quiet that I heard
a white shiny snowflake drifting from the sky.
It was so quiet that I heard
a slimy snail coming to the flowerpots.
It was so quiet that I heard
a clear tear coming down on my face.
It was so quiet that I heard
a black spider making a shiny web.

Tyler Young (7)
SS Peter & Paul's Catholic Primary School, Lichfield

It Was So Quiet

It was so quiet that I heard
a tinkling snowflake falling from the sky.
It was so quiet that I heard
a beautiful rainbow shining.
It was so quiet that I heard
a sad tear dropping.
It was so quiet that I heard
a shiny twinkling star.
It was so quiet that I heard
a ladybird crawling across the floor.
It was so quiet that I heard
a crawling spider spinning on its web.
It was so quiet that I heard
a snail slithering.
It was so quiet that I heard
the clouds waiting to be filled.

Matilda Markantonakis (7)
SS Peter & Paul's Catholic Primary School, Lichfield

It Was So Quiet

It was so quiet that I heard
a tiny ladybird flicker across my face.
It was so quiet that I heard
a rainbow spreading its colours across the sky.
It was so quiet that I heard
the dazzling raindrops pittering and pattering.
It was so quiet that I heard
the fluffy clouds floating across the sky.
It was so quiet that I heard
people scratching and screeching their pens across the page.
It was so quiet that I heard
someone sharpening their pencil.
It was so quiet that I heard
someone rubbing their work out.
It was so quiet that I heard
Miss Simons ripping the sticker off the roll.

Katy Nash (7)
SS Peter & Paul's Catholic Primary School, Lichfield

It Was So Quiet

It was so quiet that I heard
a running tear dripping on my face.
It was so quiet that I heard
a little ant crawling on the floor.
It was so quiet that I heard
an ice cube melting in my cup.
It was so quiet that I heard
a shiny star spinning up in the sky.
It was so quiet that I heard
the whistling wind.
It was so quiet that I heard
a scratch on the door.
It was so quiet that I heard
the wind blowing.
It was so quiet that I heard
a dog running.

Hannah Wright (7)
SS Peter & Paul's Catholic Primary School, Lichfield

Bethany

She is as funny as a comedienne
Punk rock as a rock star
Soft as a pompom
Dramatic as a drama queen
As smiley as a cartoon on TV

As fashionable as a fashion queen
As clever as a professor
As weird as a four-legged snake
But she is my best friend.

Evangeline Ford (10)
St Benedict's Catholic Primary School, Atherstone

David

He's a hell boy,
A funny clown,
He's a Vincent van Gogh,
He's the greatest creator,
A famous novelist,
He's a jolly puppy,
He's a cool magician,
He's a good friend.

Kieran Forsyth (10)
St Benedict's Catholic Primary School, Atherstone

Alicia

She is full of warm bubbles
She's a very soft cat
She's an extremely cool cucumber
She is a funny clown
A jolly sailor
Great fun to have around
A good friend.

Rachel Burns (9)
St Benedict's Catholic Primary School, Atherstone

Ryan

He's a hopping rabbit,
He's a big batter,
He's football mad,
A cricket bat,
A smelly rascal,
A dope,
He's my best friend.

Tyler Beeson (9)
St Benedict's Catholic Primary School, Atherstone

Miss Harrold

She's a McDonald's,
She's a lily,
She's a fun clown,
A fabulous toy,
She's a netball post,
She's an orange ball,
She's a piece of silk,
She's nothing but beautiful,
A great computer,
The sound of a fountain,
A cute kitten.

Tiana Cavanagh
St Benedict's Catholic Primary School, Atherstone

Holly

She's a bright sun,
She's a good paint brush,
She's a bluebell,
She's a bouquet of flowers,
A funny joke,
A parrot,
A large teddy bear,
A pile of leaves,
The sound of birds,
A Cadbury chocolate bar,
The smell of fresh bread,
She's a small spider,
A big piano,
A huge butterfly.

Ola Wrobel (10)
St Benedict's Catholic Primary School, Atherstone

Holly

She's a small whisper,
A first-aid box, always to the rescue,
An extremely grumpy Sir,
A DFS sofa,
Sunken, locked treasure,
The cutest cat on the block,
A light bulb always switched on,
A big clown,
The smell of a newly picked, freshly grown rose,
The sun,
She's a Renault Megane,
A white chocolate bar,
David Beckham's golden goal,
My shadow, always connected,
And guess what?
She's my best friend.

Heather Lees (9)
St Benedict's Catholic Primary School, Atherstone

Josh

He's Dairy Milk chocolate,
A superstar!
A mini Tim Henman,
A quick car,
He's mad about sport,
He's a bright sun,
A stubborn mule,
A tasty burger in a bun.

Daniel Morton (9)
St Benedict's Catholic Primary School, Atherstone

Grace

She's a smiling sun,
She's a clarinet,
She's a soft, comfy bed,
A musical funfair,
A jolly happy soul,
A skating banana,
A juicy pear,
An encyclopaedia,
A pencil.

Alicia Winfield-O'Hare (9)
St Benedict's Catholic Primary School, Atherstone

Nathan

He's a really fast cheetah,
He's a loud jet fighter,
He's a fierce T-rex,
A sweet lemon,
A really soft rock,
The smell of old people,
A hard school chair,
A funny clown,
He's the best.

Shannen Strugnell (9)
St Benedict's Catholic Primary School, Atherstone

Santa

He's the smell of snow,
A bright sun,
A clean vacuum cleaner,
An old potato,
As round as a bubble,
A bullet stuck in a gun.

Ryan Daly (9)
St Benedict's Catholic Primary School, Atherstone

Jamie

He's a mad dog,
He smells like an apple,
He's the FA Cup,
He's a cricket bail,
A tall giraffe,
He sounds like a rhino,
He's a tasty chicken,
A scratchy monkey,
A smooth blade of grass.

Jonathan Strugnell (9)
St Benedict's Catholic Primary School, Atherstone

Kieran

He's a sunny day,
A radio station,
He's a tasty ice cream,
A mint bush,
He's a rubber,
He's a yo-yo,
He's a hot air balloon,
He's a chip.

David Tremlett (9)
St Benedict's Catholic Primary School, Atherstone

My Friend

She's a comfy pillow,
She's a vibrating chair,
She's a set of drums,
A lemon sherbet,
A demanding puppy,
A tasty bar of chocolate,
A secret diary,
A text book.

Abbie Palmer (9)
St Benedict's Catholic Primary School, Atherstone

Harriet

She's a ball in a goal,
She's a very ripe kiwi fruit,
She's a springy jack-in-a-box,
She's a bouncy strong rabbit,
An aquamarine dolphin,
The new netball champion,
The season of fall,
Every colour of the rainbow,
A fluffy squishy pink marshmallow,
A never-ending book,
The tallest, most yellow sunflower,
The pop of a cork flying out a champagne bottle,
A know-it-all whizz-kid.

Lucy Turner (9)
St Benedict's Catholic Primary School, Atherstone

Josh

He's an entertaining clown,
He's a sizzling sausage,
He's a cricket game on a PlayStation,
He's a tasty chip,
He's mini Rooney,
He's fudge cake,
A smelly salmon,
A fast bolt of lightning,
He's a radio,
He's a small K Pieterson,
He's a donkey,
He's a snappy crocodile.

Jamie Dorman (9)
St Benedict's Catholic Primary School, Atherstone

Heather

She's a balloon full of bubbles,
She's a cute brown rabbit,
She's a colourful mask,
A bullet stuck in a gun,
The taste of a chicken nugget,
A computer,
The smell of a beautiful rose,
The sound of a bird in the morning,
The feeling of silk,
A Komodo dragon,
A scrumdiddlyumpcious Wonka Bar,
A weeping willow,
She's a very good . . . friend!

Holly Paton (10)
St Benedict's Catholic Primary School, Atherstone

Mr Hammond

He's a helping robot,
He's a football,
He's a detective,
A sarcastic clown,
The super electric guitar,
A soaked surfboard,
A loud roaring tiger,
A windy fan,
He's the taste of a juicy cheesy wheezy cheeseburger.

Zak Yates (9)
St Benedict's Catholic Primary School, Atherstone

Lucy

She's the cheekiest monkey in the zoo,
She's the best chocolate in the box,
She's the winning goal,
The ripest banana in the bowl,
Better than Picasso,
The biggest fish in the sea,
A Neapolitan ice cream,
The smell of a fully bloomed rose,
A book with all the answers,
A raspberry smoothie,
A happy sun,
The happiness that fills my heart,
A megaphone,
A hairy yeti,
The pot of gold at the end of the rainbow.

Harriet Littlewood (9)
St Benedict's Catholic Primary School, Atherstone

My Nan

She's a vacuum cleaner,
She smells like a rose,
She's a supermarket,
The sound of a sponge on a dish,
The touch of velvet,
A motorbike,
A sparkling sea,
A tasty strawberry,
The best nan in the world.

Patrick Davey (9)
St Benedict's Catholic Primary School, Atherstone

Abbie

She's a fresh glass of fizzy sparkly lemonade,
The sound of a huge old elephant trumpeting,
A mad, mischievous, cheeky monkey,
A bright, colourful, talkative parrot,
An active, healthy athlete,
A funny entertaining clown,
The taste of fizzy sour sweets,
The smell of a fresh morning,
The touch of a fluffy teddy bear.

Rosie Holland (9)
St Benedict's Catholic Primary School, Atherstone

My Brother

He's a playing piano,
He's a sour pear,
He's a pair of football boots,
The smell of a new football kit,
The sound of drums,
A rough doormat,
The taste of banana,
He's a mini Ronaldo,
A Christmas Day full of laughter.

Chloe Smith (9)
St Benedict's Catholic Primary School, Atherstone

Santa

He's a melting dairy chocolate bar,
He's a quiet secret agent,
He's a big, shiny, red football,
He's a huge, white, fluffy sheep,
He's a loud zooming car,
The strongest muscle man in the universe,
The smell of the oldest, dustiest Christmas tree,
A loud cheeping falcon flying to the sun,
He's a bright light bulb,
He's the best.

Sophie Skelcher (9)
St Benedict's Catholic Primary School, Atherstone

A Poem About A Dog

A huge Great Dane
Galloping down the road
Got scared by the pussycat
And fell on a toad.

A tiny Chihuahua
Hopping down the road
Tripped and jumped
Upon the toad.

A great fat puppy dog
Plodding down the road
Was being very silly
And lay on the toad.

That poor toad
Was having a really 'ruff' day!

Caitlin Price (9)
St Francis Xavier's RC Primary School, Hereford

A Victorian Child

Feeling sad and alone
Walking down the street
Nobody cares.

Nobody wants me
Nobody feeds me
Nobody loves me.

Nowhere to sleep
Nowhere to lay down my tired head
Why was I born God?

Shaun Miller (10)
St Francis Xavier's RC Primary School, Hereford

School Sounds

It was so muffled that I heard . . .
The bin sigh
As the rubbish came in . . .

It was so muted that I heard . . .
The book flap
Like the wing of an eagle . . .

Simon Chapman (8)
St Francis Xavier's RC Primary School, Hereford

The Mutated Creature

A giant mutated creature
Was walking down the lane
He got hit by a ICBM
And he was never seen again.

Jack Doyle (9)
St Francis Xavier's RC Primary School, Hereford

I'm A . . .

I'm a cute little pony,
Trotting down the road,
I saw a pretty mare
And switched to love mode.

I'm a sweet little Kiwi,
Climbing up a rope,
I did a big flip,
With a lot of hope.

I'm a really little bird,
Flying in the sky,
I flew into my cage
And landed in pie.

Kathryn Morrison (9)
St Francis Xavier's RC Primary School, Hereford

A Handful Of Precious Jewels

In my hand I hold . . .
A ruby like a deep red rose,
An emerald like a peacock's feather,
A sapphire like the glittery blue sea,
An amber stone like the golden sun,
An amethyst like lavender incense,
A milky-white opal like a glowing candle
And a diamond shimmering like the silver moon.

Martha Willson (10)
St Francis Xavier's RC Primary School, Hereford

A Victorian Child

A sad, lonely, weeping child,
Lying upon the ground.
A soul of sadness
A body so brittle.
No home, no family,
A place where there is no food.
Dense in mud.
Ill with diseases,
Rickets, polio, so many more.
Pure hell for the children.
Dark, dingy alleyways in which they sleep.
Feet are blistered so badly it's hard for them to walk.
Factories or mines are death traps for children.
Very little pay,
Keeps the food coming in little by little.
From morning till night children just sit there
And watch people pass by.
People who think they're superior look down at the children
And give them looks like dirt on their shoe.
No one would help them.
Tears in their eyes.
Clothes made of rags.
No smile comes upon them,
No mother or father to brighten their day.
Poor, poor Victorian child.

Bryony Reed (11)
St Francis Xavier's RC Primary School, Hereford

Evacuee Child

Last week on a smelly, noisy train.
Five days ago on a bumpy bus.
Four days ago walking, painful feet.
Three days ago getting used to a new family, tricky.
Yesterday buying sweets, using coupons.
Today working, exhausting.

Dominic Fawcett (9)
St Francis Xavier's RC Primary School, Hereford

A Victorian Child

I am a slave, young and weak
I gasp for air and struggle to speak.
From five 'til eleven I am a sweep
For the next few hours I just sleep.
They shove me up chimneys, narrow and black
And if I am late, I get given the sack.
Sad and cold in my dark alleyway
There are things about me I cannot say.
I'm aching and lonely here in my box
And when I pick pockets, I'm sly as a fox.
All I wear is a tiny rag
When the rich boy walks past, all he does is brag.
I used to be a miner, full of diseases
I'm better now but the aching never ceases.
I am a slave, young and weak
I gasp for air as I struggle to speak.

John Lloyd-Williams (10)
St Francis Xavier's RC Primary School, Hereford

A Victorian Child

A sad, lonely, tired child
Working all day long
No home to go back to
Just a candle and a piece of bread
Sweeping chimneys, sweeping chimneys all day long
No food, no drink, just work, work, work!
Dust in my throat and up my nose
Nasty sneezing all day long, can't stop, can't stop!
It hurts so much but I have to carry on
I wish I could go home now
But I have to carry on or else I will get whipped
I really want to stop! My arms are hurting,
I think they are breaking and my legs as well
But I know if I get sacked I will get no food and die
So I have to carry on!

Amy Sadler (10)
St Francis Xavier's RC Primary School, Hereford

Invasion Of London

1940, nearly midnight,
Clouds expand,
Crashing planes,
Thunder screams,
Fearlessly, pilots jumping from planes.

Whirring sounds echoing through the black bleached skies,
Bits of shrapnel flying,
Planes skipping in the skies,
Blinding searchlights,
Fire blazing through the engines.

Ear-splitting sounds,
Now the end of London.

Max Celie-Bone (8)
St Francis Xavier's RC Primary School, Hereford

A Victorian Child

Lonely, sad
I hate this workhouse
I wish I could leave
I wish I could die
Long hours
Blistered feet
Sore hands
Hungry stomach.
Where is love?
Where is happiness?
Where is my mum?

Francis Cairney (10)
St Francis Xavier's RC Primary School, Hereford

A Recipe For An Enjoyable Day In Bed

(Inspired by 'A Recipe for a Magical Day at the Seaside' by Andrew Collett)

Take one soft relaxing bed,
Grab lots of pillows and blankets,
Toss in some delicious chocolates,
Chuck in a big bottle of Fanta and a cup,
Switch your TV on to your best channel
But make sure that you fling in some videos and DVDs.

Snuggle up in the soft blankets,
Puff up the pillows,
Open the delicious chocolates carefully,
Unfasten the bottle of Fanta and pour it into the cup.

Finally watch the videos and DVDs in bed
And eat the delicious chocolates and drink the Fanta
For the rest of the afternoon.

Catherine Bridges (10)
The Grove Junior School, Malvern

The Haunted Castle

(Inspired by 'A Recipe for a Magical Day at the Seaside' by Andrew Collett)

Find a large and empty town,
With no one but you.
Place a massive haunted castle
And a ghost or two.

Receive hairy spiders
To make your test fair.
There might be a lot of spooky sounds
So you need to be aware.

Twisting corridors
Will make you think.
Be careful of the black sand
Or you'll sink.

Hannah Murphy (9)
The Grove Junior School, Malvern

Football

(Inspired by 'A Recipe for a Magical Day at the Seaside' by Andrew Collett)

Find a large open space
Paint some clear, white lines with a ruler
Then grab a fantastic team like Man Utd
Put some magnificent players in
Like Ronaldo, van Nistelrooy and Rooney
Get a mystical manager, Sir Alex Ferguson will do the job
Go to the best ever league, the FA Premier League
But also make sure you have a football to play the great game
Have a super season and finish in the top 4
Then you will go into the greatest cup ever
Finish in the top 2 and go into the knockout rounds
Score some extraordinary goals and be top scorer
Your goalkeeper must be good like Peter Cech
Or Van der Sar
Your defence has to be in top shape
Also, your midfield has to be fit
Make sure your strikers can score goals
And most importantly enjoy the game.

Lewis Doyle (9)
The Grove Junior School, Malvern

A Recipe For Being A Good Friend

(Inspired by 'A Recipe for a Magical Day at the Seaside' by Andrew Collett)

Take a boy or a girl, make sure you like them,
Meet their friends, help her or him with their work.
Spice up with some humour and just get along together.

Finally make sure he or she isn't bossy and laugh all day long.
Sink in some friendship.
Surprise them by doing something really special
Then just take your friend and play.

Matthew Haron (9)
The Grove Junior School, Malvern

Birthday

It's my birthday,
I'm having a party,
with paint and pens,
we are going to be arty.

It's my birthday,
a lot of post,
I read my cards,
as I'm eating my toast.

It's my birthday,
don't want today to end,
I walk down the street,
and turn the bend.

It's my birthday,
I'm having fun,
as I am eating,
a big iced bun.

It's my birthday,
I am now ten,
next year I will be,
eleven like Ben.

It's my birthday,
I get ready for bed,
on my pillow,
I put my sleepy head.

Mollie Withey (9)
The Grove Junior School, Malvern

How To Win A War

(Inspired by 'A Recipe for a Magical Day at the Seaside' by Andrew Collett)

Find an opposing kingdom
With a lot of useful land
Make sure you outman them
And challenge them with your band.

Prepare your army's weapons
And polish their armour well
Make sure they all have horses
And a lovely place to dwell.

Place them in a battle
The archers on a hill
Put the arrow on the bow string
And then you can fire at will.

If it's a losing battle
Retreat to where you live
Sit there and hope and hope
There's a chance that they might give.

If it seems you're winning
Smile and fight with lust
And when it all prevails
Shout with glory, you must.

Now weary warrior
Rest your head
Because you just might win
If you do what I've said.

Jacob Chester (10)
The Grove Junior School, Malvern

The Decorated Garden
(Inspired by 'A Recipe for a Magical Day at the Seaside' by Andrew Collett)

Find a large open space,
Add a triple sprinkle,
Square water fountain,
Blue, pink, yellow and orange.

Add a stony pond,
With bright-coloured fish
And dark green frogs.

A tree house with orangey-red leaves
And brown ripped branches
And on the top of the tree,
Grow juicy fruit and veg.

Scatter flowers all round the coloured,
Decorated garden,
An explosion of colours will fill the air.

Jade Conway (9)
The Grove Junior School, Malvern

A Wonderful Garden
(Inspired by 'A Recipe for a Magical Day at the Seaside' by Andrew Collett)

Find a large space
Add a wooden tree house in a tall, bright tree
Choose a pond with fish that are free
Have a water fountain that sprinkles with joy
Make green, dark bushes out of statues
Then get a bunch of colourful flowers
And plant them in a row
Spread light green grass on the ground.

Elyshia Harpin (9)
The Grove Junior School, Malvern

The Little Warrior

(Inspired by 'A Recipe for a Magical Day at the Seaside' by Andrew Collett)

Place the warrior in his castle,
give him his weapons,
put his water, fire, leaf, thunder, darkness
and light stones in his pouch to give him courage.
Teach him his spells
place his armour on his body
and let the battle begin.

The sorcerer will summon his demons
he will take his best fighters and put them on their dragons.

Tell the water, fire, leaf, thunder, darkness and light warriors
to help him win the battle.
Grab the sorcerer's army and put it on the battlefield.
Make your army charge, fight, win.

Fraser Gordon Brown (9)
The Grove Junior School, Malvern

Romantic Meal For Two

(Inspired by 'A Recipe for a Magical Day at the Seaside' by Andrew Collett)

Find a large quiet restaurant
Add a rose or two
Make sure there's a flickering light
A candelabra or a single light
Sprinkle the starched white napkins
On each side
Choose a well-kept menu
With elegant italic writing
Search for a violinist
Add a couple
The perfect meal.

Jessica Booton (9)
The Grove Junior School, Malvern

The Fantastic Garden
(Inspired by 'A Recipe for a Magical Day at the Seaside' by Andrew Collett)

Find a space on the bright green grass,
Place a pond with beautiful plants,
Plant a tree with twisted vines
And plant some lovely flowers.
Have a stony path,
Have a maze made of a hedge
In the middle have a water fountain.
And there you are,
A *fantastic* garden.

Jessica McIntosh (9)
The Grove Junior School, Malvern

A Recipe For A Plain Lazy Day At Home
(Inspired by 'A Recipe for a Magical Day at the Seaside' by Andrew Collett)

First take a comfy sofa,
Mix in a giant American sandwich,
Season with a widescreen television with 800 channels,
Gently sprinkle in a bit of gaming,
Add some big sundaes,
Dim down the lights, put your feet up and snooze.
Finally relax and chill out!

Alice Prothero (9)
The Grove Junior School, Malvern

Autumn Colours

A golden medal won in a race in 2005,
A red dazzling rose lying in the golden sun,
A wooden tree trunk in the sun all day,
A yellow sun lying there until it goes to sleep.
Orange rustling leaves lying on the floor all day.

Owen Lancett (7)
The Grove Junior School, Malvern

Harvest

(Based on 'Magic Box' by Kit Wright)

I will put in the box . . .
The fire of the sun shining on our world
The rain falling on the flourishing crops
The wind as strong as the storm clouds
The shiny sheaves of corn from the shimmering golden fields.

I will put in the box . . .
The sight of waves of wheat bending in the wind
The sight of sweet apples swinging on the trees
The sound of juicy pears dropping to the earth
The happiness of hungry souls finally going to eat.

I will put in the box . . .
The love of the farmers' labourers looking after our land
The shining eyes of the fisherman on the silver seas
The pickers plucking olives from the glistening groves
People like us picking plump vegetables for our harvest feast.

Class 5R
The Grove Junior School, Malvern

Yes

(Inspired by 'Yes' by Adrian Mitchell)

Galaxy says: Planets
Hurricane says: Twist
Thermometer says: Heat
Tummy says: Meat

Heart says: Veins
Roads say: Separate lanes
Planets say: Mars
Sky says: Stars

Door says: Open me
Handle says: Close me
Orphan says: I need money
Bees say: Honey.

Victoria Henshaw (10)
The Grove Junior School, Malvern

The World Says

(Inspired by 'Yes' by Adrian Mitchell)

A smile says: Happy,
A heart says: Love,
When the rain says: Water,
The earth says: Dove.

The kangaroo says: Jump,
Giraffes say: Crunch,
A bus says: Pump,
While a car says: Bunch.

Lemon trees say: Sour.
A jug says: Glug,
The villain says: Power.
The Hero: Hug.

The river says: Flow.
The moon says: Yellow.
The stars say: Goodnight.
The sun says: Hello.

Emily Parker (10)
The Grove Junior School, Malvern

Places

(Inspired by 'Yes' by Adrian Mitchell)

Villages say: Welcome
Cities say: Traffic jams
Towns say: Shops
Streets say: Prams.

Forests say: Unwelcome
Rainforests say: Wet
Woods say: Log cabins
Trekking says: Set.

Sand dunes say: Scorching sand
Snow-capped mountains say: Climb
Plains say: Animals
Deserts say: Limited time.

Georgia Brittain (10)
The Grove Junior School, Malvern

Our Garden

(Inspired by 'Yes' by Adrian Mitchell)

The garden says: Plant.
The sparrows says: Day.
The owl says: Night.
The kitten says: Play.

Photographs say: Memories.
A tree says: Climb.
A seed says: Nourish me.
The herb garden says: Thyme.

Ants say: Work.
Bees say: Honey.
Butterflies say: Flutter.
The sun stays sunny.

The bindweed says: Wrap around.
The sunflower says: Follow the light.
The nettle says: Be careful.
The hedgehog says: Sleep tight.

Imogen Quilley (10)
The Grove Junior School, Malvern

What They Say

(Inspired by 'Yes' by Adrian Mitchell)

A handshake says: Hello
A brains says: I'm thinking OK!
When the sun says: Burn
The flowers say: Water me.

The jungle says: Trees everywhere!
The plants say: We are cold in the winter
The rivers says: Flood, come on
The desert says: Dry, dry, dry!

Richard Cook (10)
The Grove Junior School, Malvern

Yes

(Inspired by 'Yes' by Adrian Mitchell)

A handshake says: Hello
A brain says: Information
When the sun says: Yellow
The flowers say: Pollen.

The elephant says: Stride
Parrots say: Who's a pretty boy?
A bicycle says: Ride
While a train says: Tickets.

Palm trees say: Sway
A bucket says: Water
The cowboy says: Good day
The pop star says: Join in.

The jungle says: Gorillas
The garden says: Flowers
The icy rivers say: Shivers
The desert says: Sandy.

The Queen says: I rule
The orphan says: Rags
The thief shouts: Jewels
The fireman says: Fire.

The puddle says: Splash
The mountains say: Echo
The teacher says: Ten minutes left
The child says: Tag.

Danielle Drew (10)
The Grove Junior School, Malvern

The Planet

(Inspired by 'Yes' by Adrian Mitchell)

The tiger says: Hungry
The gazelle says: Dead
Moonlight says: Shine
The sun says: Rise

Fire says: Burn
Food says: Cook
Volcano says: Boil
Lava says: Spurt

Devil says: Blood
Angel says: Heal
Serpent says: Submerge
Surface says: Wave

Dragon says: Fire breath
Ground says: Scorch
Cherry says: Pluck
Birds says: Eat.

Robert Middleton (10)
The Grove Junior School, Malvern

Water Is . . .

(Inspired by 'What is Pink?' by Christina Rossetti)

Water is a stream,
Calm and quiet.
Water is a tidal wave,
Fast and gigantic.
Water is a liquid,
Cool and refreshing.
Water is a snowflake,
Cold and beautiful.
Water is ice,
Smashing as it falls.
Water is a tear,
Sad and small.

Thomas Hodgetts (10)
The Grove Junior School, Malvern

Rabbit

A cabbage lover
A grass nibbler
A noisy squeaker
A foot thumper
A speedy runner
A carrot muncher
A nose sniffler
A fox hater
An ear flopper
A golden digger
A cute sleeper
A straw snuggler
A water drinker
A platinum jumper
A mouse hater
A Leah lover
A sawdust sleeper
An eye glistener
A cage liver
An attention seeker
A rabbit food eater
A guinea pig friend!

Leah Henney (10)
The Grove Junior School, Malvern

Spooky House

(Inspired by 'A Recipe for a Magical Day at the Seaside' by Andrew Collett)

First get a horrifying castle
And put some scary bats
To fly around people's hats.
Add some ghosts and make the door creak.
Put an old fat mouse inside the dusty crack to make it squeak
And stomp very hard to make cracks on the path.

Jenna Holden (9)
The Grove Junior School, Malvern

Dog Kennings

A night howler
A hair maker
A dirty eater
A food waster
A stick fetcher
A playful runner
A thirsty drinker
A noise maker
A cat chaser
A good sniffer
A bone digger
A hole maker
An annoying barker
A sheep rounder
A great hearer
A loving pet.

Charmain Pearce (10)
The Grove Junior School, Malvern

Autumn Poems

Dark brown leaves falling down on me,
Red poppies standing proudly,
Oranges hanging down low.
Golden sun shining down on me,
Yellow bananas hanging from a gigantic tree,
Red gleaming traffic light flashing on and off.

Emma Pitt (7)
The Grove Junior School, Malvern

Dog Kennings

A thirsty drinker
A night howler
A tail waver
A hairy maker
A noise barker
A nose sniffer
A stick chaser
A cat eater
A ball player
A speedy runner
A hole digger
A bone finder
A food waster
A sheep rounder
An excellent hearer
A loving pet.

Ka-Kei Mo (10)
The Grove Junior School, Malvern

Autumn Poems

Cosy red heart beating softly.
Shining gold metal, beautiful and incredible.
Gorgeous yellow tulips swaying from side to side.
A shining orange wooden floor sparkling in the sunset
Falling brown leaves blowing off the trees.

Anthony Eyles (7)
The Grove Junior School, Malvern

Water Is . . . ?

(Inspired by 'What is Pink?' by Christina Rossetti)

Water is hail
That batters your head.

Water is a pond,
Soothing and cool.

Water is ice,
It's always concealed.

Water is rain
That trickles down your back.

Water is a sea
That flows and bubbles.

Water is a puddle
That you jump in and get wet.

Water is snow
That sounds crinkly and crunchy.

Water is a waterfall,
White and vicious and sometimes transparent.

Water is a flood,
Bursting with violence.

Water is a drink
That gushes down your throat,
Tasty and refreshing.

Daniel Waite (10)
The Grove Junior School, Malvern

The Waterworks

(Inspired by 'What is Pink?' by Christina Rossetti)

Water is a lake,
Remote, deep and cold
Frozen in winter,
Warm in summer.

Water is snow,
Crunchy, white and soft
Jump into it and
Gradually sink in.

Water is condensation,
Damp, frozen and moist
Press your hand to the glass
And let it get wet.

Water is a tear,
Small, round and warm
Hidden beneath your eyes
Ready for a storm.

Water is a river,
Twisting, turning and wet.
Sometimes long,
Sometimes short.

Water is a flood
Powerful, treacherous and devastating
It can happen
Anytime.

Water is a thing
We use every single day.
Wet, helpful and good to have . . .
We need water!

Helen Stevenson (11)
The Grove Junior School, Malvern

Why Be A Tree?

Fish, fish, glorious fish,
They will grant you only one wish.

I wish to be a tree,
Why a tree?
Just a tree for me.

A tree because I can feel the air,
On my hair
And get a scare,
From a polar bear.

Fish, fish, glorious fish,
I wish to be a tree,
I wish!

Rachel Beasley-Suffolk (10)
The Grove Junior School, Malvern

The Magic Box

(Based on 'Magic Box' by Kit Wright)

I will put in the box . . .
The sound of a heart breaking
The horn of a dinosaur
The smoke of a cigar

I will put in the box . . .
The swish of a magician's cloak
A little girl's life flashing
The sound of a mirror crashing

I shall write in my box . . .
The creaking of the paper as I turn the page
The sharpness of the pen as it hits the paper
The eyes focused on the page.

Zoe Evans (10)
Whittington CE Primary School, Worcester

A Skeleton At The Bottom Of The Sea

(Based on 'Fishbones Dreaming' by Matthew Sweeney)

A skeleton lay on the seabed.
He was a pirate, with a gun and map.
Soon there would be nothing left.
He didn't like to be this way.
He shut his eyes and dreamt away
Back to when he was a good pirate.
When he worked beside Black Leg Bill
And slept on the top hammock.
When he scrubbed the decks,
Till his hands were wrinkly.
He didn't like to be this way.
He shut his eyes and dreamt away
Back to when he was on Treasure Island
Where he buried their treasure.
Five months they were there.
He didn't like to be this way.
He shut his eyes and dreamt away
Back to when he worked at the Seaside Pub,
With Sam Long and also Big Black,
In the kitchen of the pub.
Where he found a treasure map.
He didn't like to be this way.
He shut his eyes and dreamt away
Back to when he was a little boy,
When he lived with his uncle
And he went to school.
Or when he stole a pistol from his uncle.
He liked to be this way.
He dreamt hard to try and stay there.

Alice Fisher (10)
Whittington CE Primary School, Worcester

Alphabet Zoo

I'd like to introduce to you
The crazy creatures from the alphabet zoo:
An agitated anaconda attacking ants,
A barmy bison bellowing Beethoven,
A crunching cobra considering constricting,
Devious dragonflies destroying documents.
An excitable echidna eating earwigs,
Fantastic fruitbats flying fearsomely,
A gorgeous giraffe galloping gamely,
A horrible hog, headbutting hedgehogs.
An inquisitive iguana investigating insects,
Jealous jaguars jousting jackals,
A kipping koala kissing kiwis,
Leaping lemurs loop-the-looping,
A marvellous moose munching mushrooms.
A nauseous newt napping noisily,
An outrageous orang-utan ogling oranges,
Peckish piranhas pulverising prawns.
Quivering quails queuing for Quavers,
A rampaging rhino roaring ravenously.
A snoozing sloth soundly snoring,
Terrifying termites trying to topple towers,
Undersea urchins undulating unusually.
A venomous viper viciously vibrating,
Wishful warthogs wandering woefully,
An extraordinary extinct xenotarsosaurus exiting,
A yelling yak yodelling, 'Yippee!'
Zany zebras zooming zoologically.
And so we say, 'Farewell, adieu!'
To the crazy creatures in the alphabet zoo.

Rory Wilkinson (10)
Whittington CE Primary School, Worcester

Senses Poem

I like to touch
The furry coat of a dog,
A spiky hedgehog,
The small silky body of a hamster,
A fluffy cat on a chair.

I like the taste of
Sweet and sour chicken sliding over my tongue,
Hot dogs from the barbecue,
Delicious chocolate that melts in my mouth.

I like the sounds
That I can hear properly with my hearing aids,
My dad saying hello,
People talking in the street as I walk past.

I like to see
The pretty flowers when I visit my grandad's,
The adventures of Scooby-Doo.

I like the smell of
Bacon sizzling in the frying pan,
My mum's perfume,
The smoke from burning fires floating in the air.

Daniel Burch (10)
Whittington CE Primary School, Worcester

A Sense Poem

I like to touch
The popping bubbles in my bath.
A soft silky cat.
The prickly spikes on my dad's head.
A very silky dog.

I like the smell of
Oil in the pan spitting as the sausages go in.
The leather of a new football.
My dad's aftershave.

I like the sound of
Foxes screeching in the night.
Birds in the morning.
The loud music of the Gorillaz, my favourite band.

I like the taste of
Sour mints exploding in my mouth.
A fluffy Yorkshire pudding filled to the top with gravy.
Fizzy pop and Pringles.

I like to see
Foxes gobbling food in the dark garden.
People working hard.
The town on Saturday bustling with shoppers.
My mum's smile on a Sunday morning.

Tom Massingham (10)
Whittington CE Primary School, Worcester

The Magic Box

(Based on 'Magic Box' by Kit Wright)

I will put into the box . . .
An anaconda's nerves,
An aeroplane's propeller
And the colour of a sunset.

I will put into the box . . .
The football boots of Frank Lampard,
The first computer ever made,
The day Thomas Edison made the light bulb.

I will put into the box . . .
The Leeds United football pitch,
The most strict teachers in the world
And the cleverest person ever known to man.

My box will be decorated with gold, silver and bronze,
Its hinges are a phoenix's talons
And the padlock's code is the Ten Commandments.

I will fly in my box
Over the Earth and far away,
Go to the red planet of Mars
And explore everything humans have never explored before.

Ryan Upson (10)
Whittington CE Primary School, Worcester

The Magic Box

(Based on 'Magic Box' by Kit Wright)

I will put in the box . . .
A moonlit sky with twinkling stars,
A tooth from a hare
And a claw from a beast.

I will put in the box . . .
The wrinkles from my grandma,
The smell of garlic bread,
The sound of a river running by.

I will put into the box . . .
Steam from a kettle,
Three wishes from a fairy,
The eye from a snake.

I will put into the box . . .
A fin from a whale,
The colour of ink from an octopus,
A cry from a baby.

My box is fashioned from jade, amber and ruby,
With ruby diamonds formed as flowers,
With jade and amber hinges and locks.

I shall read in my box,
I shall put in talent,
A little bit of imagination,
I will put all the characters in my box.

Jade Morris (10)
Whittington CE Primary School, Worcester

Carrot Shredding Dreaming

(Based on 'Fishbones Dreaming' by Matthew Sweeney)

Carrot Shredding lay on the wooden chopping board.
All that was left was a few peelings of his beloved body.
Soon the mopping cloth would sweep him into the bin.

He hated to be this way.
He shrivelled up and thought back.

Back to when he was a thin orange stick.
Side by side with a few peas and a sliced piece of celery.
With two greasy hands picking him up,
Shoving him into one great big jaw.

He hated to be this way.
He shrivelled up and thought back.

Back to when he was captured in a plastic bag.
In the freezing cold fridge.
Singing a song at the bottom of the bag.

Back to when he was purged at the bottom of the basket.
With a hundred other carrots curling up
Hoping someone wouldn't pick them up and buy them.
Carrot Shredding was peeling off the sharp points in the basket.

He hated to be this way.
He shrivelled up and thought back.

Back to when he was cosy in the moist soil.
Every day a tall man came and gave Carrot Shredding water.
The cool breeze gave Carrot Shredding a gentle kick to grow.
He was surrounded by all his friends.

He absolutely adored it to be this way
So he shrivelled up and imaged he was there.

Josh Clayton (10)
Whittington CE Primary School, Worcester

The Magic Box

(Based on 'Magic Box' by Kit Wright)

I will put in the box . . .
The sound of a sea washing upon a shore,
Fire from a dragon's puff,
The touch of cotton wool.

I will put in the box . . .
A leaping rabbit swimming in the sea,
A unicorn with a mouthful of cheese,
A bubble floating in the sky.

I will put in the box . . .
The venomous bite of a spider,
The colour of the wind,
And the gleam of the sun shining in the sky.

I will put into the box . . .
A talking tree in the winter breeze,
A flying panda holding a shark
And a sting of a jellyfish.

My box is fashioned from flowers, hearts and sand,
With dogs on the lid and coconuts in the corners.
Its hinges are the knees of a kangaroo.

I shall fly in my box
Over the high peaks of Mount Everest,
Then sail onto clear water
The colour of the sky.

Charlotte Mitchell (10)
Whittington CE Primary School, Worcester

Paper Dreaming

(Based on 'Fishbones Dreaming' by Matthew Sweeney)

Paper lay in a recycled bin
He was creased and painted
Soon he would be crushed up in the dustbin van.

He didn't like to be this way
He folded up and dreamt away

Back to when he was in a little child's greasy hands
And was being painted with a really stiff paint brush
That hurt him all over.

He didn't like to be this way
He folded up and dreamt away

Back to when he was taken from an opened packet
By a lady who was talking to herself
And laid on the smooth hard bed.

He didn't like to be this way
He folded up and dreamt away

Back to when he was in a sealed packet
In a big house where lots of people came to take you away,
He was with a lot of friends.

He didn't like to be this way
He folded up and dreamt away

Back to when he was out in the open
And with his family and friends
And everybody who walked past saw him being happy.

He really liked to be this way
He tried to fold up and stay this way.

Emma Sheldon (10)
Whittington CE Primary School, Worcester

I Will Put In My Box

(Based on 'Magic Box' by Kit Wright)

I will put in my box . . .

The face of the Earth,
The smoothness of a grape,
The taste of Lambrusco wine.

I will put in my box . . .

A candyfloss cloud up in the sky,
The sound of bubblegum being chewed,
A leaping spark from an electric fish.

My box is fashioned from . . .

Ice, all things good and a black sun.
With stars in the corner and flowers on the lid.

I shall ski in my box

Down Mount Everest
Drop into a pool at freezing point
And swim with the dolphins across the Atlantic.

Kieran Rodway (10)
Whittington CE Primary School, Worcester

Heart Of Gold

The man next door
His name is Fred
He wears a tea cosy on his head.
He walks really slow
While his red nose is aglow.
He moans and groans
And will never answer the phone.
He just sits and watches telly
Eating rhubarb and jelly
Whilst resting the TV remote on his belly.
But so I have been told
He's got a heart of gold
And will do anyone a favour
So I'd say that makes Fred a fab neighbour!

Paige Jones (10)
Whittington CE Primary School, Worcester

Pollution

Squashed cans in the streets
Bottles broken and smashed
In rivers and streams.
Scrumpled up crisp packets
Thrown on the pavements.
Fish and chip shop newspaper
Blowing about all smelly and greasy.
Supermarket bags caught up in hedges.
The rivers are full of horrible things flowing,
Slithering down in the water.

The trolleys, acid, smoke,
Pollution.

Jodie Kerton (9)
Wigmore Primary School, Wigmore

Pollution

Crisp packets flying around the streets,
Crushed cans picked up by the wind and tossed around,
Squashed plastic bottles trapped in drains,
Rubbish rolling out the bins with the wind,
Chewing gum squashed on pavements.
Fire burning bright letting smoke run free, destroying our world.
Fridges abandoned in ditches deserted by their owners.
Trolleys put in rivers drowning under the waves.
Mattresses dumped in rubbish tips.
Glass shattered on the floor cutting children as they fall.
An acid rain falling, burning leaves.
Food wasted put in bins, then in junkyards.
I see plastic bags on pavements, roads and in rivers.
I also see oil bottles bobbing on top of the waves.
Bombs exploding in the cities and towns.

James Phillips (9)
Wigmore Primary School, Wigmore

The Rubbish Truck

Hey, don't mess with me,
I'm the big green rubbish truck from down the street.
I'm burping up toxic gases
And chewing, chewing up babies' nappies.

I'm loaded with fossil fuels
I'm burying rubbish
I'm adding to the greenhouse
I'm heating up the Earth.

If I were smaller maybe it would change
The pollution in the air will die like old rain
Maybe it will, when I'm 100!
If we don't act soon who knows what will happen!

The world is in danger from global warming.

Lexine Maughfling (10)
Wigmore Primary School, Wigmore

We Are The Energy Wasters

Water gurgling down the drain
Litres and litres at a time.
Eating energy.

Kettle frothing
Ready to explode,
Too much water for one cup.
Eating energy.

Lights blazing
But there is no one at home.
Eating energy.

Heat escaping through the walls,
Rushing out the open doors.
Eating energy.

TV blaring, who's watching?
It's an empty room.
Eating energy.

Washing machine pumping water
For a single shirt.
Eating energy.

Cars spitting out smoke
That's more carbon dioxide,
For the greenhouse effect.
Eating energy.

What is happening to our planet?
We are wasting energy every day.
Eating energy.

Hannah Mason (10)
Wigmore Primary School, Wigmore

Wasting Energy

Cars drinking petrol and diesel
Every minute coughing it all out,
Through the engine,
Pumping out poisonous gases.
Polluting the atmosphere.

The washing machine
Guzzling down water
Faster than the speed of light,
Shooting through the pipes to be disposed of.

Lights eating up electricity
Lighting up an empty room,
Wasting energy for no one.

The heater giving away heat
Letting it drift out of open doors and windows,
Wasting energy like there's no tomorrow.

Television showing for no one
Energy being wasted.
What is the point?
We're destroying our future.

Alex Edwards (10)
Wigmore Primary School, Wigmore

The Wind

Trees blow in the breeze
Their branches bend and rustle
On a blustery autumn day.

The swirling leaves
Twisting, dancing as they fall
On a gusty autumn day.

Jamie Bufton (9)
Wigmore Primary School, Wigmore

Rubbish Dump

We treat our world like a rubbish dump.
Empty, squashed,
7Up and Coke cans.
Lying on the streets,
Bottles - broken and smashed.
In rivers and streams,
Empty crumpled up crisp packets.
Fish and chip newspapers blowing about.
Smelling and bad and greasy.
Supermarket bags caught up in hedges.
At sea, oil spills of mini rainbows of poison.
It's rubbish isn't it?

Thomas Stevens (9)
Wigmore Primary School, Wigmore

There's A Something

There is something in the bed,
I wonder what it can be?
It has only just arrived,
So I'd better go and see.

I glanced all around me,
What is this mess I see?
There's something in my bed
And it's staring back at me.

It has chucked off the pillows,
Tossed about the sheets,
Messed up all my clothes
And eaten all my sweets.

Oh! It is only my puppy.

Hannah Segar (8)
Wigmore Primary School, Wigmore

What A Waste

Acid rain burning trees and forests,
Smashed bottles in drains, hedges and on roads.

I smell chemicals and smoke,
Polluting and killing.

I smell fire, keeping us hot and heated,
Empty Coke cans squashed and left lying around in hedges.

I smell chemicals and smoke,
Polluting and killing.

Ripped, torn, plastic bags float in rivers and streams,
Smashed cars abandoned and left on roads and streets.

I smell chemicals and smoke,
Polluting and killing.

Sticky chewing gum squashed into pavements and sticking to walls,
Sewage smells horrible, polluting rivers.

I smell chemicals and smoke,
Polluting and killing.

What a waste!

Zak Kyriakou (9)
Wigmore Primary School, Wigmore

Octopoem

A teacher is multicoloured,
She is the autumn,
In the classroom
She is sunny,
A teacher is a polo shirt,
A desk,
She is the news at 10 to 10,
She's bacon, egg, beans and potatoes.

Sam Boxhall (8)
Wigmore Primary School, Wigmore

Pollution

Acid rain rushes down and destroys the tree leaves.
Oil spills like a flowing river.
Sewage runs under the huge cities making ghastly smells in
our streets.
Chemicals race to our crystal clear sea and turn it revolting colours.
People throw trolleys and washing machines into rivers
and in our clean environment.
Lots of pollution rushes out of dirty, disgusting factories
into our bright blue skies.
Fag ends stuck in gutters and pots.
Forest fires kill a lot of trees, animals and much more.
Petrol spills in the ocean like whales swimming for life.
The filthy factory smoke seeping out of chimneys.
Chemicals sloshing into our gently flowing rivers.
Seas polluted by jet-black oils.
People chop down our trees in the forest.
Pieces of wood float down the rivers like mini boats.
Bits of metal scattered everywhere.

How can we help?

Kirsty Ann Gibbs Mellings (9)
Wigmore Primary School, Wigmore

Millie

I have a friend called Millie
Who really looks quite silly!
She's got a flowery hat,
Like Grandmother's cat.
She's got a drippy nose,
Like a leaking garden hose,
She's got big wide eyes,
Like she's just had a surprise.
She's got golden-brown hair,
Like a toffee apple at the fair.
Yes, Millie is a sight to see,
But she's as kind as can be!

Jake Pontifex-Price (8)
Wigmore Primary School, Wigmore

Trash

Oil polluting the crystal clear sea,
Making rainbow patterns,
Killing fishes.

Acid rain falling from the grey, ugly sky.
Killing glistening green leaves and trees.

Smoke is a killer.
Whenever you breathe in,
It swirls into your lungs, choking you.

Empty beer bottles smashed
Lying in dirty alleyways cutting feet.

Cars abandoned in streets,
Rusting and rotting in rivers,
Slashed tyres causing floods.

Ripped up newspapers floating around like ghosts,
We live in a trashy world and it's everyone's fault.

Rhys Brown (9)
Wigmore Primary School, Wigmore

Gilly

I have a friend called Gilly
Who is as strange as can be!
She's got long curly hair
Like a brown woolly bear.
She's got deep, dark eyes
Like big fat pies.
She's got a tiny round nose
Like the bud of a rose.
And a long thin chin,
Like a screwed up tin.
She's got sweet little ears
Like fairy tears.

Jack Lewin (8)
Wigmore Primary School, Wigmore

Energy

There's a lot less to energy than you think,
It is wasted in just a blink!
Once it's gone it won't come back,
Fossil fuels, there is a lack.

Let's start on lights, they are the worst,
In a wasting competition, they'd come first!
Lights in the bedroom, lights in the hall,
Anyone would think we were having a ball.

Taps wasting water, there just isn't point,
By taking a bath to only wash your joints!
Same with cars, but they pollute the air,
This causes a greenhouse effect,
But some people don't care.

There's a lot more to energy than you think,
It is wasted in just a blink!
Once it's gone it won't come back,
Fossil fuels, there is a lack.

Emma Crooke (10)
Wigmore Primary School, Wigmore

Lights

Lights on the computer screen, nobody playing!
Lights in the streets when nobody's around,
Lights in the shop window, nobody working!
Lights on the TV screen, nobody watching.

Lights in the bathroom but nobody there,
Lights in the dining room, nobody eating!
Lights in the living room, nobody laughing!
Lights in the bedroom, nobody sleeping!

Lights in the porch, nobody leaving!
Lights in the kitchen but nobody's cooking,
Lights in the hallway, no visitors arriving!
Lights in the garden, nobody chatting!

Lucy Brown (10)
Wigmore Primary School, Wigmore

Save Energy

Lights burning for nobody,
TV watching itself,
Radio dancing to itself,
Dishwasher cleaning nothing,
Cars rumbling for petrol,
Hot water turning cold for nobody,
Heaters making themselves warm,
Computers playing games,
Kettles making a cup of tea for themselves to drink,
Planes wasting petrol just to go on holiday,
Tumbledryer drying clothes that do not need to be dried,
You need to stop wasting energy,
Stop leaving TVs on,
It is your future,
You may think the greenhouse effect is not that bad,
But it is,
You will want to go back when we had energy
So stop using energy.

Siri Lewis (10)
Wigmore Primary School, Wigmore

Some Feelings

There is something in the air
I wonder what it can be?
It's only just arrived
So I'd better go and see.

It's tingling and tickling
Snow is floating from the sky.
Do you know what it is?
It's the feeling of January.

I love the summer days
When pink blossom lights up the trees,
I pluck strawberries from a bush
Lazy, hazy days.

Sophie Hatt (8)
Wigmore Primary School, Wigmore

What A Waste

Lights blazing for no one,
What a waste!
Hot water left running, feeling lonely,
What a waste!
Heat flooding out of wide open windows,
What a waste!
Kettle with a bulging belly for just one cup,
What a waste!
Computers sitting as still as stone,
What a waste!
Dishwasher spilling water,
What a waste!
Washing machine spinning round frantically,
What a waste!
Cars spilling out petrol onto a tarmac road,
What a waste!

Lucy Willmett (10)
Wigmore Primary School, Wigmore

My Friend Millie

I have a friend called Millie
Who really looks quite silly!
She's got hair of wire
Like the colour of fire.
She's got ears that twitch
Like a dog with an itch.
She's got a bright red nose
Like paint on your toes.
She's got big round eyes
Like chicken pies.
Yes, Millie is a sight to see,
But she's as kind as can be!

Olivia Edwards (8)
Wigmore Primary School, Wigmore

Trashed-Up World

Acid rain falling from the sky
Burning holes through the green leaves on the trees,

Rivers full of beastly chemicals, rubbish and car wheels
And all sort of objects,

Smashed, rusty cars abandoned in the middle of nowhere
Trapping poor animals inside,

Oil spills making rainbows in puddles
May look pretty but very deadly,

Bottles, cans, plastic bags, crisp packets
Can trap a lot of animals, especially birds
And it causes a lot of pollution.

Dusty, rusty washing machines dumped in a wood,
Trashed-up just like their crashed doors broken off for good,

Fridges getting abandoned left standing at a slant,
Watch out, the doors might close, *slam!*
No air left.

If we don't act now there will be no happiness left.

Phillipa Yarranton (10)
Wigmore Primary School, Wigmore

In The Wood

Deer dashing, dodging through the trees
Dancing, prancing as it comes,

Jumping over the shimmering river,
Galloping out of the wood.

I race to see what it is doing,
I see the deer catching a butterfly.

I watch it fade away into the moonlight,
Then fall asleep on the window sill
And my dreams are filled with deer!

Lucy Evans (8)
Wigmore Primary School, Wigmore

Lights

Lights in shop windows, nobody's gazing.
Lights in bedrooms, nobody's playing.
Lights in the kitchen when nobody's there.
Lights are left on because nobody cares.

Lights are screaming, 'Turn me off when you leave the room!'
Lights are shouting, 'One day we'll go *boom!*'

Lights are shining in the street.
Lights are beaming when everyone's asleep.
Lights in the bathroom when nobody's there.
Lights are left on because nobody cares.

Lights are pleading, 'Please turn us off!'
Lights are crying, 'We're attracting the moths!'

Anastasia Hince (10)
Wigmore Primary School, Wigmore

The Jockey

A jockey is dark brown,
He is the spring,
In the stable,
He is hail,
He is joddies,
He is a wheelbarrow,
He is the Grand National,
He is runner beans and steak.

A jockey is amazing,
He is a star,
Jockeys are really horsey,
Jockeys are the best!
I want to be a jockey.

Serena Reid (8)
Wigmore Primary School, Wigmore

Energy

Televisions flicker hoping to be watched.
The TV's stallions, leaping for victory.
Computer switching the plug, can it succeed?
In the midst of the Internet, sprinting with speed.

Lights munching the energy.
Flickering, wasting away . . .
Wave goodbye to oils,
As coal recoils.

Kettles overflowing onto the floor.
Taps spitting water into the bath.
The electricity provided by gases.
As the flames burn and time passes.

The smell reaches the highest points.
Gives the greenhouse effect more power,
Scorching the Earth, to a crisp.
Covering the Earth in a smoky wisp.

Aaron Meadows-Skuse (11)
Wigmore Primary School, Wigmore

Dinosaurs

The dizzy diplodocus danced,
Dotting and dashing in the disco.

The vicious velociraptor played violins
Eating breakfast with vegetables.

The crazy coelophysis
Cooked chilly cod.

The tyrannosaurus
Trotted along tricking troodons.

The egg-stealing oviraptor
Acted very oddly.

Luke Bingham (8)
Wigmore Primary School, Wigmore

The Washing Machine

A big eye staring at you as you walk around the kitchen,
Gargling water around in its throat,
Eating energy, eating energy,
Frothing at the mouth after drinking a cappuccino,
Water trickling down its arm, soothing its hot throat.

Clothes drowning in the depths, fighting for air,
The machine whirrs with greed,
Eating energy, eating energy,
Whizzing round like a roundabout,
Stirring up the underpants.

Sucking up electricity,
Guzzling our supplies,
Eating energy, eating energy,
Wasting our fossil fuels,
Being burnt just for me.

Dad's dungarees,
Swishing skirts,
Stinky socks,
Ugly underpants.

Are clean clothes more important than our planet!

Kayleigh Mumford (10)
Wigmore Primary School, Wigmore

Mrs Edwards

Mrs Edwards is orange,
She is the autumn,
In the classroom,
She is warm,
Mrs Edwards is a ballgown,
Mrs Edwards is a solid wooden desk,
She is the news,
She is a big box of Thorntons *chocolate!*

Bethanne Harris (8)
Wigmore Primary School, Wigmore

Car

Climbed in the car,
Car coughed,
Engine spluttered,
Wheels twisted.

Car starts up,
Car screams,
Car speeds down the driveway,
Doesn't stop.

Petrol dripping,
Lights shining,
Stops at petrol station,
Drinks petrol.

Car races down the road,
Then brakes screech,
Waiting for traffic lights to turn green,
Car parks in the driveway.

Petrol pumps from the car
Making a puddle,
Ready to stop.

Fossil fuels dying away,
Never to be replaced,
What is happening to our world?
We're wasting energy.

Nicola Luscott (10)
Wigmore Primary School, Wigmore

Fear

Fear is grey
It tastes like cold ice cream
And smells misty and old,
Fear looks like a hooded witch,
The sound of slow footsteps,
Fear is dark.

Abbigail Beamond (8)
Wigmore Primary School, Wigmore

Pollution

Old rusty metal shopping trolleys
swirling down the river.
Pollution

Ripped, empty, dirty, scrumpled-up crisp packets
stuffed into hedges.
Pollution

Scruffy, ripped-up newspaper
chucked on the floor.
Pollution

Acid rain
falling from the sky like fire.
Pollution

Forest fires as
red as blood.
Pollution

Chemicals are as dangerous
as a charging rhino.
Pollution

Chemicals dashing past huge
rocks like a ball of fire.
Pollution

Trolleys, crisp packets, newspaper,
acid rain, forest fires.
Pollution.

Harriet Hodnett (9)
Wigmore Primary School, Wigmore

Pollution

Acid rain destroying forests
Chemicals oozing into dirty smelly rivers,
What a waste.
Oil spills polluting crystal clear water
What a waste!
Car fumes belching out of exhaust pipes
Burning up the ozone layer right now
What a waste
What a waste!
Scrunched up crisp packets swirl around in rivers,
What a waste.
Smelly, dirty, rotten cars
Rust in ditches, what a waste,
What a waste.
Litter, litter on the ground
Cans,
Cars,
Bags everywhere
Pick them up if you dare!
What a waste.
I smell smoke in houses tall, in open spaces
Large and small.

Harry Martin
Wigmore Primary School, Wigmore

The Washing Machine

A big eye staring at you as you walk around the kitchen.
Gargling water around in its throat.
Frothing at the mouth after drinking cappuccino.
Water trickling down its arm, soothing its hot throat.
Water whizzing around like a merry-go-round.
Washing being eaten by a metal machine,
Chewed up, ripped, swallowed, gobbled up.

Emma Bevan (10)
Wigmore Primary School, Wigmore

The World Is A Rubbish Tip!

Use the bin, don't dump and throw your litter on the floor,
Use your brain; you'll hurt our world if you drop anymore!

Cars belch out sooty grey fumes and exhausts,
As they drive on a road made of chewing gum and litter.

Litter growing in trees, and plastic bags in bushes,
Then blowing away with the leaves in autumn.

Crashed, smashed, bashed cars dumped and
Abandoned on roadsides,
Left, left to trap small animals, to injure deer and badgers.

Chemicals oozing over stones in brooks,
Sliding past crisp packets and sweet wrappers
And escaping into a crystal clear sea.

Use the bin, don't dump and throw your litter on the floor,
Use your brain; you'll hurt the world if you drop anymore!

That's what I call *pollution!*

Laura Johnson (9)
Wigmore Primary School, Wigmore

The Old Car

The engine splutters and gurgles to life.
Chug, chug.
The wheels twist and turn as it runs down the road.
Chug, chug.
The car is screaming, up on the line is a dead rat.
Chug, chug.
The car looked at his home, next to the garage was a new car.
Chug, chug.
The old car had gone for sale, 'Please buy me,' he said.
Chug, chug.
Now there are two cars wasting fuel and making smoke.
Chug, chug.

Agnes Pierzynorrska & Alice Hughes (10)
Wigmore Primary School, Wigmore

Wasting Our Energy

The water swishing down the drain,
Running down the pipes, feeling lonely.
Filling up the kettle for one cup of tea or coffee.

Watching the water washing the clothes,
Seeing the water gurgling through the holes,
Staring at the clothes being scrunched up,
Seeing an eye glaring at you.

Light bulbs burning electricity,
Glaring at an empty room alone.
Wasting electricity.
Please turn off the lights.

Fossil fuels wasting away,
Wasting away,
Never to be replaced,
So don't waste them.

Leaving heating on
When no one's in the room.
Turn it off.
Don't waste energy.

Cars roaring,
For just one person.
Leaking petrol,
All over the ground.

Sophie Moore (10)
Wigmore Primary School, Wigmore

Energy

There's a lot less to energy than you think,
It's wasted in just a blink!
Once it's gone it won't come back,
Fossil fuels, there is a lack.

Let's start with lights, they are the worst,
In a wasting competition, they'd come first!
Left on when there's no one there,
Brightening a room for just the air.

There's a lot less to energy than you think,
It's wasted in just a blink!
Once it's gone it won't come back,
Fossil fuels, there is a lack.

Let's go to the washing machine,
Wasting so much energy, just to keep our clothes clean!
Not just energy, water too,
Even worse than the loo!

There's a lot less to energy than you think,
It's wasted in just a blink!
Once it's gone it won't come back,
Fossil fuels, there is a lack.

Rhiannon Probert (10)
Wigmore Primary School, Wigmore

Love

Love is rosy-pink
It tastes like butter icing cakes.
Love looks like a giggling bouncing baby.
Love smells like a bunch of new-grown flowers
And a flower bed garden.
It sounds like children playing in the playground.
Love is best.

Jasmine Hodges (8)
Wigmore Primary School, Wigmore

Energy

Computers flicking and flashing waiting for someone to use them,
Wasting energy
Washing machine spinning hot water around to wash your clothes,
Wasting energy.

Lights flickering and burning away all through the night,
Wasting energy
Huge loud stereos blasting out music for no one,
Wasting energy.

TVs blaring out to armchairs sitting all alone,
Wasting energy
Kettles full up to the brim, for one cup of tea,
Wasting energy.

Cars guzzling gallons of petrol
For one person to drive,
Wasting energy.

Stacey King (10)
Wigmore Primary School, Wigmore

Energy

Lights burning,
Kettle whistling,
Computers raging all through the night,
Cars starting up all the time,
Washing machine going round and round,
TV, radio and stereo blaring all the time,
Cars, trains, buses and planes going every hour,
Hot water being boiled, but nobody using it,
Dishwasher going *wish, wash, wish, wash*
Burning fossil fuels like mad, mad, mad,
Radiators pumping out heat,
Whole bath being filled just for a two minute wash,
Gas being left on after you finished cooking,
Wasting energy.

Robin Millward (10)
Wigmore Primary School, Wigmore

World Pollution

Terrible chemicals bursting into sparkling rivers,
How can we help?

Acid rain falling from the sky like fire,
How can we help?

Forest fires ruining habitats,
How can we help?

Rusty cars' duct tape everywhere,
How can we help?

Scrumpled-up crisp packets in the streams,
How can we help?

Chewing gum stuck on streets,
How can we help?

Mouldy sandwiches thrown in the river,
How can we help?

Chemicals, acid rain, forest fires,
Rusty cars, crisps, gum, sandwiches,
How can we help?

Lara Davis (9)
Wigmore Primary School, Wigmore

Our Dirty World

I smell fuel as I walk past the petrol station
And all it has is chemicals.
Smashed bottles lying in the gutters,
Rusted washing machines in ditches,
Cigarette ends stumped out on our pavement,
Chewing gum stuck to your shoes and on the streets.
Crisp packets all ripped and lying in alleyways,
Trolleys drowning in lakes and rivers.
Rusty cars all around us.
Bottles smashed and thrown on the ground.

Our dirty world.

Dale Williams (9)
Wigmore Primary School, Wigmore

Lights

Lights in bedrooms,
Flickering, flickering,
Lights in shops,
Blazing, blazing,
Lights in factories,
Burning, burning,
When no one's around.

Lights shining on a computer,
Lights shining on the TV,
Lights shining on a laptop,
When no one's around.

Lights in the bathroom,
When no one's in,
Lights in the sitting room,
But nobody's there.
Lights in the dining room,
When no one's eating.
Nobody's at home.

Lights are screeching,
To be turned off.
Lights are pleading,
To have a rest.
Lights are crying,
To stop being used so much.

Nobody cares about waste!

Iona Reid (10)
Wigmore Primary School, Wigmore